*Loneliness,*
*Solitude,*
*and Companionship*

# *Loneliness, Solitude, and Companionship*

## ROBERT E. NEALE

THE WESTMINSTER PRESS
*Philadelphia*

*Book design by Alice Derr*

*First edition*

Published by The Westminster Press®
Philadelphia, Pennsylvania

PRINTED IN THE UNITED STATES OF AMERICA
9  8  7  6  5  4  3  2  1

**Library of Congress Cataloging in Publication Data**

Neale, Robert E.
   Loneliness, solitude, and companionship.

   1. Loneliness—Religious aspects—Christianity.
2. Solitude—Religious aspects—Christianity.
3. Fellowship—Religious aspects—Christianity. I. Title.
BV4509.5.N43 1984      248.8′6      83–26065
ISBN 0–664–24621–4 (pbk.)

# CONTENTS

## SOLITUDE

## COMPANIONSHIP

# PREFACE

This book is about our adventures in relationships. Sometimes we are separate and lonely, like an infant who has lost and seeks its mother or like a dying old man who has no family or friend to care. Other times we are alone, but not lonely, like a lover whose memory and anticipation in solitude discovers the bond to his beloved even more clearly in her absence. And then there are those times of companionship when our engagement—between husband and wife, man and dog, or woman and God—is supportive and yet challenging. It is this movement from one condition to another which constitutes our adventure. Our relationships are movements between loneliness, solitude, and companionship.

When we see the liveliness of these adventures, we may be amazed at the richness of our living, but also confused and frightened. Why are our relationships, supposedly as natural as breathing, so difficult and unnatural? If we are so embedded in relationships, why do we feel so lonely? And must our companionships so complicate our lives? Tempted by self-pity, we complain about having to choose between two hells—the loneliness of isolation and the vulnerability of connection. But to be both separate and together is our lot. Because of the uncertainty and change it engenders, we are prompted to discover ourselves, those to whom we relate, and the relationships themselves. If we can tolerate being just a little bit amazed, or confused, or frightened at the liveliness of our relationships, we can explore these adventures with the possibility that depth and fullness will increase.

Our exploration involves both theory and application. I will offer
theories about loneliness, solitude, and companionship. They spring
from my attempts to understand my relationships, and I apply them
to myself. I expect you to do likewise. We need not worry very much
about whether the theory is true. But I hope we do worry about
whether we can use it to further our self-understanding. What is
interesting is not relationship in general, but my relationships and
your relationships. So the theory is accompanied by exercises that
suggest ways of applying the insight to yourself. Mechanically, all
you need is a pencil and paper. But no exercise is self-working. I hope
that you will not read this book in one sitting, seeking only the
opinions of authorities, or reflecting only on the relationships of
others. Rather, you should take your time, read a chapter, and reflect
on yourself fully before continuing. The content of each chapter has
been used by many small groups of students and others of all ages.
Such sharing with others can sustain and enrich our private reflections. But whether alone or with others, we are to explore, not theory
alone, but ourselves by means of theory.

Exploration requires courage, because it is usually prompted by
perception of a problem. In our case, it will happen mostly when we
experience separation, loneliness, and hopelessness. At these times,
we wonder if we have ever really known anybody. And have we?
Really? Have we really known our parents or our children? Our
lovers or our friends? Have we known anyone fully? Will we ever?
We are strangers. Which one of us is not always a stranger to others?
Forever a stranger. This is our situation. To explore it takes courage.
In looking at our own mood of loneliness, we will be anxious. But
by examining also what loneliness is and why we are lonely, we will
conclude that it is as valuable as it is disturbing. In looking at our
solitude, we will see our desire to be alone and have done with others.
But we will also discover that solitude is discovery of relationship
and that it has as much to do with others as with ourselves. We may
then turn with relief to the comfort of companionship, only to realize
that it is not the final goal and resting point of relationship, but a part
of the process that returns us to loneliness and solitude. The need for
courage remains. There is a kind of death in loneliness, a kind of
gestation in solitude, and a kind of rebirth into companionship. But
we find ourselves traveling through these stages over and over again.
Because of this travel, the familiar becomes unfamiliar. Relationships
change. Therefore, relationship is always with the strange. No per-

son, no object, no God is ever totally familiar. So we must have considerable courage to begin and to maintain our exploration.

We will have surprises. That is, we will encounter something strange in ourselves, in others, and in the relationships. What will surprise you? How will you respond? These encounters with the strange are the payoffs we should hope for. I hope that you will be compassionate toward these surprises, welcoming them into your self-reflections. I hope that you will employ them for your own learning. And I hope that you will find them awesome, so much so that they compel you to develop your relationships. Such compassion, employment, and awe are the elements of hospitality—the welcoming of strangers. Strangers we will remain, but we can welcome each other. Let us try to do so.

Because this book is a response to my own experiences of relationship, I am indebted to all those I have used in my reflections. I have been reminded of relationships with family and relatives, friends and colleagues in various professional, avocational, and community groups, and persons from many of the generations of humankind. In addition, I have been reminded of relationships with objects and animals and other things of nature and of our creation, and of relationship with the world as a whole. If you are like me, you are forgetful of the sheer number of relationships that are important to you. The reminder of them has been rewarding for me, as it would be for you. I can mention only a few.

A few of my family and relatives: my father and mother, Hugh and Nell Neale; my brother Hugh, his wife, Arlene, and their children, Geoff, Charles, and Peter; my grandmother, Mabel Clark; my aunt, Frances Clark; my former wife, Margo; my children, Becca, Dave, and Doug; friends of my parents, the Hirts, Lehners, Nickels, Noes, and Steehs.

A few of my friends: from childhood and adolescence, Eddy Bowers (imaginary), Johnny Buckley, Lyle Biersdorf, Wyatt Mick, Mary Carolyn Wright, Bill Weller; from young adulthood, John Keydel, Don Koessel, Phil Alexander, Wally Anderson, Robin Roth, Monte Miller; from more recent beginnings, Dutch Rosenberger, Clarence Collins, Sam Randlett, Louise Goss, Jane Keydel, Lillian Oppenheimer, Persi Diaconis, Karl Fulves, Tom and Marion Frazier, A. J. and Hank Levinson, Bernie and Luciana Steinzor.

A few of my mentors and colleagues: from high school, Sam Barbakoff, Temp Licklider; from college, Al Martin; from seminary, Bob Brown, Dave Roberts, Bob Seaver, Edgar Jackson, Earl Loomis, Jack Greenawalt, Gene Laubach, Bob Lynn, Larry LeShan, Will Gaylin, Ann Ulanov.

A few whom I have not met directly: Rembrandt, Jesus, Marcel Duchamp, Paul, Mark Twain, Luther, Emmett Kelly, Freud, Van Gogh, Jung, Jimmy Durante, Harry Stack Sullivan.

A few of my student colleagues, those from my first course on loneliness: Trudy Brown, Eve Edmond, Allen Grooms, Roger Hawkins, Bob Heinle, Ralph Hicks, Ruth Mullis, Ruthmary Pollack, Martha Postlethwaite, Katharine Shinn, Lee Sullivan, Sharna Sutherin.

A few of my things: from childhood, wagon, tree in the backyard, rock collection, field by the river, Jimmy and Champ (dogs); from adulthood, the Vermont summer camp, Kemo (dog), every single one of all my books, collection of paperfolds, two houseplants.

Two of my symbols of the world as a whole (excluding some of the people and things mentioned above) are idiosyncratic devices: broken cross, toy ball gimmicked to have neither inside nor outside.

I am aware of many others I have not mentioned, and I have undoubtedly forgotten still others. To all these I am indebted, pleased to be so, and grateful for having been reminded of my connections.

As for my typist, Gail Potter, she happens also to be my teddy bear, source of new relationships, image of the Great Mother, and my friend.

# Loneliness

# CHAPTER I

## *Recalling the Mood*

We begin exploration of relationship by recalling our own experience of loneliness and the accompanying mood. Stop reading silently for a moment and say the following words aloud and very slowly: lone · . . . alone . . . lonely . . . lonesome . . . aloneness . . . loneliness. The sounds stimulate a mood connected with our vague memories, feelings, and thoughts about lack and loss of relationship. We will note first the courage required for us to explore this mood, then do our own personal exploration, and finally reflect upon our reactions.

Thinking about loneliness requires courage. Speech appears to fail us. What is doubtless a powerful experience of loneliness can be rendered rather flat in communication.[1] Why so? The limitations of speech reflect the limitations of our courage. Loneliness baffles clear recall because we are so frightened by it.[2] Do you not, right now, sense some anxiety, or the possibility of some anxiety, regarding your own experience of loneliness? It is understandable that we are not prone to talk about it, or to be rather toneless if we do. And do you not have some moments of sheer loneliness that you have forgotten about gladly? If you do remember some of these experiences now, ones that you did not recall earlier, you are very likely to disconnect them from your present self. We say to ourselves, "Yes, I suppose I was lonely, but I wasn't myself then."[3] When we are lonely, we may have quite a different organization of emotions and self-understanding than when we are not lonely. This different self, the lonely one, is considered to be other than and alien to our normal self. The mood of loneliness is not welcome. To recall the mood is to be recalled into it, and this is quite unwelcome. Our exploration requires courage.

There are, however, explorations of loneliness that do not require great courage. We need not try for consciousness of the worst moment of loneliness in our own lives. There are two alternatives. One is to explore our more minor events of loneliness. Since separation occurs over and over to each of us, and since loneliness is the most natural and common reaction to separation, all of us have been lonely, and been so repeatedly. Just mention this topic to anyone you know and you are likely to hear the reply, "Oh, I'm an expert on that!" What is fortunate, for the sake of our pleasure and our recall, is that the degree of loneliness has varied considerably. A woman leaves her family to visit relatives for a few days. The husband misses her and feels lonely. A schoolchild is sick in bed with the flu. The child misses the social life with peers and feels lonely. Such low-level loneliness is bearable and subject to recall. It is easier for us to sense the mood in such cases than in the extreme loneliness that may occur with a death, divorce, or transplantation from one culture to another. However, we who seek such deliberate recall may be surprised that the "minor" experience was more powerful than previously acknowledged. The mood of loneliness cannot be controlled, even when recalled with relative safety.

We are not limited to exploring our own loneliness in this direct fashion. The second alternative to recalling our worst loneliness is to be reminded of it by stories of other lives. The loneliness of certain heroes, such as Jesus of Nazareth or Lincoln of Illinois, is a tool by which we both confront and support our own experience. Probably most of us have personal heroes, informal saints who are symbols of what is important to us. We use fiction and drama similarly, the loneliness of a Hamlet or Arthur Miller's Willie Loman helping us both to perceive and to support our own experience. The public lives of civil rights leaders such as Martin Luther King, Jr., Hollywood stars such as Elizabeth Taylor, musicians such as Ringo Starr, and celebrities such as Jacqueline Kennedy can remind us that we are not alone in our loneliness. Quite beyond words and persons, we may seek out the experience in paintings, such as self-portraits of Van Gogh, and in music, such as the late works of Tchaikovsky. The stories of other lives and their contributions are gateways to the mood of loneliness that we can tolerate and use.

Without these alternatives of exploring our minor experiences and the experiences of others, it is doubtful that we could deliberately encounter the mood of our own loneliness at all. Perhaps it is true that we can rarely explore our own loneliness in absolute isolation. For when we recall it, we are thrust into the experience of loneliness again. Willfully to seek such recall without a sense of being connected to and sharing with another human being would be too painful to bear. Quite possibly, exploration of our own loneliness can occur only when we believe that it is, at the same time, at least partially overcome. To share loneliness is to limit it. Even to read about another person's experience as reflected in a novel is to enter into a community that counters the loneliness evoked. Of course, recall of our loneliness can and does occur even without such an attenuated community. Such recall is, undoubtedly, unsought and serves only to increase the mood of loneliness. It is no wonder that we seek to avoid it. We need courage, and a leading source for it is community.

The time to begin our deliberate exploration of our own experience and mood of loneliness is now. Take pencil and paper and write at the top of the sheet of paper: "My Own Loneliness." Write a statement of no more than one hundred words on a personal experience of loneliness. You have only these few words to tell the event in story form. Do not worry about spelling, grammar, or literary merit. Take a minor experience from your past, an experience that is not too powerful because it is small and old. Finally, I suggest that you select an experience you would not mind sharing with anyone else. Take ten minutes to do this. Do it now before reading any farther.

Having taken this first step, you might be interested in what others have written. Here are just two examples:

> The first evening returning to boarding school after the spring vacation. The snows were melting, the ground was muddy from thawing, yielding the smell of damp, dank earth, the drab appearance of my dormitory room, the sound of chirping "peepers" from the nearby swamp. The wave of the feeling of loneliness came over me as I thought of warm family and home which I had left a few hours before.

> I lived in a new community in a house by myself. After a month, I got a baby monkey for a pet. During the day, he was frightened of me, but during the

night, he slept beside me to keep warm. After six weeks he got used to me. Then I had to leave him overnight. When I came back, he was dead. I buried him. That night I cried and cried, just bawled on and on more than I ever have as an adult, before or since. Only then did I realize how lonely I had been and why I wanted a pet.[4]

After reading these stories, read your own again. If you like, read these stories to someone else and suggest that the person write a story of personal loneliness that you can read. Or if you are a member of a group doing this exploring, be sure that everyone has a copy of all the stories that have been told. These stories are basic data for our understanding of loneliness. Keep them so they can be referred to at any point in your reading of this book.

We are not yet finished with this first exercise. Our recollection of an experience of loneliness has given rise to feelings and thoughts. A mood has risen of its own accord. What is your own mood? One way to get at this is to think of a single word that depicts it. Then, think of any other word that does the same, and then another. This can be done most easily in a small group. If the words are called out and written on a blackboard, all in the group are stimulated by the variety of responses, and the number and variety are greatly increased. But you can do this by yourself. Do so now. At the bottom of the sheet of paper telling about your experience of loneliness, write a single word that suggests the mood. It can be an abstract term, such as "yearning," or it can be a concrete and metaphorical term, such as "clammy." Think of one word and write it down. Now, take another three minutes to write down whatever other words come to mind. Do not evaluate them. Do not exclude anything that comes to mind. Just write whatever words occur to you.

Having done this follow-up exercise, you might be interested in what others have said about the mood. People doing this exercise have said: numbness, choking, yearning, annihilated, entrapped, deserted, sadness, black, bitter, greasy. These are some of the feelings and thoughts we may associate with loneliness. When small groups of people have been asked to work together on a statement about the mood, they say:

A feeling of panic, helplessness, deep pain and emptiness, a sense of longing—particularly a longing to be touched, either physically or spiritually, as if the touch itself would heal.

Loneliness is late afternoon, walking on a foreign street on a foggy morning; busy telephone lines; a newspaper blowing down an empty street; a howl from a mountain; sitting in the midst of people in a library; going home and no one's there; a fog.[5]

After reading these lists and groups of words, reread your own words for the mood of loneliness. Are there any additions you want to make? If so, take a moment to write them down.

For the concluding part of this exercise, we turn away from our own experience and use the stories and contributions of others. We are concerned with persons and things that depict the mood of loneliness for us. The persons can be real or fictional, and the objects can be of any kind. These categories are deliberately vague so that you can have no constraints on your awareness. Now turn your sheet of paper over and make two lists. At the head of the first, write "Person," and at the head of the second, write "Object." Note down in a word or phrase the persons or objects that depict loneliness for you. Remember that no justification is required. There is no right or wrong. You may not ever be able to say why a certain person or object depicts loneliness for you. That is perfectly all right. The important thing is to make the two lists. Do so now. Take five minutes only.

Again, you might be interested in what others have put in their lists. The list of persons has included: Jesus on the cross, any old man on a city bench by himself, people in *The New Yorker* stories, crowds, Harry Truman when deciding about the bomb, Marilyn Monroe, my sister, Job, Malcolm X, adolescents in Salinger's stories. The list of objects has included: stray dogs, Robert Frost's poem "The Road Not Taken," paintings of the sea, a painting by Edward Hopper, words and music of the Beatles, empty streets in a big city, discarded stuff —litter, deserted buildings, dead trees, anything in a rummage sale. As before, reread your own list and make any additions prompted by the items mentioned above. When this is done, you have finished your first exercise.

We began by commenting on the limitations of words to communicate the mood of loneliness. Perhaps they are not so limited. Probably the words of your loneliness event and the lists of persons and objects are quite powerful for you and for others who have heard

them. Our powerful words quickly generate loneliness. Robert Frost
can do so in a line. Speaking of an old man living in isolation on a
winter night, he records: "A light he was to no one but himself."[6] The
line exists in the very center of a poem filled with images of darkness.
To be a light only to oneself is a desolation beyond easy acknowledgment. Quite different from the quiet chill of Frost is the fiery anguish
of the psalmist. By comparison, the author of Psalm 31 shouts his
horror:

> Take pity on me, Yahweh,
>     I am in trouble now.
> Grief wastes away my eye,
>     my throat, my inmost parts.
>
> For my life is worn out with sorrow,
>     my years with sighs;
> my strength yields under misery,
>     my bones are wasting away.
>
> To every one of my oppressors
>     I am contemptible,
> loathsome to my neighbours,
>     to my friends a thing of fear.
>
> Those who see me in the street
>     hurry past me;
> I am forgotten, as good as dead in their hearts,
>     something discarded.
>                                        (Ps. 31:9–12, JB)

This lonely old man is not reserved in his expression. He has much
to complain about. He begins with grief which is perceived as an
aggressor that eats up his body and his whole life. The deterioration
is not only from old age, physiologically, but also from the accumula-
tion of all kinds of losses. The progression of losses is matched by
a progression of emotions. But the climax takes a quieter tone. The
last stanza reveals what lies at the core—separation. Loneliness is
often accompanied and covered over by many reactions which must
be explored before there can be a revelation of their primary source.
And when the revelation occurs, what can one do but resort to
Yahweh, if one is so fortunate as to believe in such an ultimate
bulwark against loneliness? Perhaps the psalmist can speak so hon-

estly of his condition because he can affirm that human existence is not ultimately lonely. For others, inner numbness is matched by the numbness of the ultimate reality. Yet the psalmist is not always so assured of the presence of Yahweh either.

These words about loneliness that we have written and read are powerful for us, assuming that we have had the courage to let them be powerful. The very request that you do the exercise might have given rise to anger or anxiety. The process of the exercise might have given rise to many feelings. Were you sad, nostalgic, bitter, joyful (yes, this is possible), angry, frightened, contemplative? It is likely that we have more than one reaction and that our reactions are contradictory. Did we wallow in self-pity? Perhaps we were surprised by lack of feeling, or overwhelming feelings. Surprise itself is one of the common reactions to the exercise, and to loneliness itself. We observe: "I didn't know I felt that way about such and such." It does take courage to allow the content and feelings to come into consciousness.

The greatest courage is required when the mood of loneliness hits us with full force. It raises the understanding that to be totally separate is to be not at all. "Am I?" This is a truncated version of "Who am I?" And this question is the truncated version of another: "To whom am I related?" When the mood rules, we can all understand the sharp cry of King Lear: "Who is it that can tell me who I am?" And when we do not know who we are, we are not. Theodore Roethke states the issue succinctly. What is the mood of loneliness?

> The feeling: you are alone in the room. If you turn
> around you will not be there.[7]

This is difficult for us to hear, so I will try again through the words of another poet, a woman who was deeply disturbed and had the courage to speak of it.

### PANIC

> And is there anyone at all?
> And is
> There anyone at all?
> I am knocking at the oaken door . . .
> And will it open
> Never now no more?

I am calling, calling to you—
Don't you hear?
And is there anyone
Near?
And does this empty silence have to be?
And is there no-one there at all
To answer me?

I do not know the road—
I fear to fall.
And is there anyone
At all?[8]

This is not a great poem. Yet when I read it aloud in the presence of others, I find it difficult to maintain my composure. I suggest that you read it aloud. Listen to your own voice saying: "And is there anyone at all?" There are moments in our lives when we do wonder about this. And properly so. The mood of loneliness is the mood of nothingness. When we are engulfed by it, we sense an active power that pursues, overtakes, and destroys. Loneliness is acknowledged by means of courage.

# CHAPTER II

## *What Loneliness Is*

The mood of loneliness is catching and enveloping. It moves from one of us to another and from one part of our lives to another. Our experience of it in the present prompts recall of past loneliness and anticipation of future loneliness. We see it as negative, lacking in pleasure and meaning. The mood may so overwhelm us that we are in confrontation with nothingness. These reactions are understandable. But just as the experience of anxiety is a most useful warning to us that there is danger to be dealt with, so also is loneliness a useful warning. And it is a warning that we can do something about. Loneliness may overwhelm us because we do not know how to see it or respond to it. So we explore it now in order to understand what it is and how it functions in our lives.

### What Loneliness Is: Separation and Search

Loneliness is usually defined as a state in which something is missing. We are aware of absence as a most powerful presence. My lack of something can influence me more than something I possess. Recall the empty chair of a loved one who is dead. The emptiness can be an overwhelming presence that rules over all else that is present. In a poem about absence in which she visits a place where she had last met a loved one, Elizabeth Jennings testifies that nothing was changed, and then says that it was precisely because of this that the absence was "a savage force."[9]

In addition to the feeling of absence, we sense that a change has taken place. Something has happened, so that we are removed from a relationship.[10] This break in accustomed connection lowers our morale; we wonder if and how we have failed, whether we are worthwhile. This preoccupation, in turn, helps to lower our coping ability; when we feel "low," we do not go about our daily activities with our usual energy. What is significant in our lives is not the sheer amount of social support we have, but sufficient regularity in relationship. We have known more loneliness in recently bereaved or divorced persons than in the long-term single person. Some of us have minimal relationships in a life-style of independence and are not lonely very much, whereas others of us who are maximally connected with others can become most lonely when separation occurs.

The change need not be an exterior one. Rather than experience the loss of a relationship by physical severance from another, we can experience an interior change that creates loneliness. This is illustrated by the growing awareness of the adolescent girl, Frankie, in Carson McCullers' play *The Member of the Wedding*. When her older brother returns home with his future bride, Frankie discovers that one can get married. She has a new understanding of the possibilities of relationship and the consequence is a new loneliness. She can say:

> The trouble with me is that for a long time, I have
> been just an "I" person. All other people can say
> "we." Not to belong to a "we" makes you too lone-
> some.[11]

The change that fosters loneliness can be this interior growth which is a discovery of possibilities of relationship.

But loneliness is more than the passive and unhappy acquiescence to separation. The other basic element is search. It is a consequence of our powerful faith that relationship is possible. Loneliness is not a passive and static condition, as the mood inclines us to believe, but a most active state.[12] It is an attempt to right the wrong of absence. We illustrate this most clearly in the extreme when strong absence is matched by strong faith. As lonely children we had imaginary playmates. We will relate socially to an idea, or to a stone if necessary. We are adaptable, wildly creative, and will find the oddest resolutions to our searching when we have to. What would some men do without their dogs? What would some women do without their God? Cats, dead heroes, trees, a poem—anything can become our companion. What would we all do without the fantasies that create some sense of relationship when none may appear for the moment or the days or the years? To whom do we talk when there is no one to talk to? I have such people in my mind and heart and I assume that you do, too. We are driven to maintain our sense of "we" by hook or by crook. The bizarre outcomes we see in others (and that others see in us) should not blind us to the strength of the inner faith that is a part of loneliness.

Loneliness may be defined as having two aspects, both of which must be present for the condition to occur: the experience of separation and the search to overcome it. Without the experience of separation, loneliness will not occur. But the separation may not lead to loneliness when we experience separation either affirmatively or with hopelessness. In neither case is there motivation for search. The combination of separation and search is lively: Loneliness is a full engagement in the struggle to participate in relationship. And since it is a common, daily experience, this struggle is a continual aspect of our lives. We tend to forget how concerned we are about relationship. The experience of loneliness is a reminder.

Before you read farther, it would be useful for you to relate the definition of loneliness to yourself. Reread your written narrative of a loneliness experience, and answer the following questions. Be brief and concrete.

1. From whom or from what was the separation?
2. For whom or for what was the search?
3. Was determining the answer to either or both of the above questions difficult? If so, indicate in what way.

The point suggested by this exercise is that the content of the experience is not always clear and simple. For example, in the narrative about the death of the pet monkey, the loneliness involved separation from the monkey, but also from others in the narrator's life. As to what others, only the author of the story could say. Because some persons and objects represent others as well as themselves, the focus of our separation and search is complex. To see fully the answers to the above questions is to appreciate the richness of our loneliness.

## Positive and Negative Aspects

Loneliness as separation and search appears to have both negative and positive aspects. Exploration of the mood of loneliness suggests to us that the experience is unfavorable in that it makes us feel bad and able to do little. But exploration of what loneliness is suggests to us that it is favorable in that it is an action toward relationship. So if our leading concern is the elimination of pain, then we can try to survive with a minimum of relationship. Our loneliness will be minor, as will be our satisfactions. But if we are able and willing to endure the pain of loneliness, we are attempting to change ourselves and/or our environment for the sake of relationship. This is a form of survival which can provide greater satisfactions. We can conclude then that loneliness in general serves a good purpose. Unfortunately it never occurs in general. In an individual case—in my case or yours —there can be so much loneliness that the mood offers only a blow to the head that shocks us to a standstill. And even when we are not so shocked, our inappropriate responses to separation and search can be damaging to relationships.

Our typical response to separation is negative. This is reasonable, because such loss is a threat to our well-being. But a chronic negative response is not useful. Separation is a reality built into our environment. Think about the course of your life and you can see it easily characterized as a series of separations. Weaning is not a once-and-for-all event, but an intermittent, lifelong process for us all. Separation, for all its danger, encourages development. How could we grow up without it?

Our typical response to search is affirmative. This is reasonable, because the threat to our well-being is acknowledged and countered. We admire ourselves and others when we know that some "doing" is happening. But a positive response to search is not always useful. Most of us know individuals who lose a spouse through death or divorce and subsequently enter into a series of quick, intimate relationships. If this promiscuous searching becomes chronic, it is probably not very useful. Have you known a bereaved person who turned only to God? This can be a discovery of a Companion who supports the loss of companions. But we can suspect also that chronic substitution of this sort may be destructive flight from possibilities of intimacy with another human being. Linking ourselves anew to another can be very useful, but a leap from loneliness to relationship can be shallow, destructive of self, and abusive of others.

We get ourselves into unnecessary suffering when we do not react to the negative and positive aspects of both separation and search. Relationship involves the self and the other one. One of these poles disappears when our responses are one-sided. For example, when separation is viewed positively and search negatively, the focus tends to be on the self only. When we believe that nothing worthwhile has been lost and nothing worthwhile can be gained, indulging ourselves becomes our only concern. "Doing your own thing" can be symptomatic of this condition. The despair is barely concealed. We all have had moments when we have said to ourselves, "To hell with them all, I'm just going to have a good time." It is useful to be able to do this, but as a chronic state of mind it is a perversion of loneliness which creates most unhappy gods.

The contrary also occurs. When separation is viewed negatively and search positively, the focus tends to be on the other pole only. When we believe that there is nothing worthwhile about ourselves, then the group can take over. Instead of glorying only in yourself, have you ever gone to the other extreme for a while, finding your own life in a group? This abandonment of self can appear in us as a concern for family, local community, church, or political movement. At worst, we live only by means of an "ism." Here also the despair is barely concealed. It is useful to be able to throw ourselves without stint into groups, but as a chronic state of mind, it is also a perversion of loneliness which creates most unhappy zombies.

Our conclusion is that we should accept the positive and the negative aspects of both separation and search. A balanced appreciation allows neither denial of separation nor despair about search, but does foster realism about the old and hope about the new. There is a time for denial and despair over relationship. They serve us well when we are overcome, enabling us to endure until other means of coping can occur. Denial and despair need to be, but need not be everlasting. We are moved quite naturally into them and then away from them toward realism and hope. Accepting both separation and search eventually works to prevent our flight from ourselves and from others. We can then remain engaged in the battle to participate in relationship. Too much loneliness creates a tension within that can destroy us. But too little allows for laxity in relationship. Courage is required so that we can let the tension increase, if necessary, and then use it for full exploration of our condition.

At this point, we return to your own narrative of a loneliness experience. Here are six more questions to consider. Be brief and concrete in your answers.

1. Which element of the experience was more prominent than the other? Separation. Search. Neither.
2. What were the negative aspects of the separation?
3. What were the positive aspects of the separation?
4. What were the positive aspects of the search?
5. What were the negative aspects of the search?
6. Which pole of the experience was more prominent than the other? Self. Other. Neither.

The purpose of this exercise is both to increase your awareness of the positive and negative aspects of your experience and to help you see ways in which you might be trying to escape or minimize your experience. Now that you have thought about the loneliness contained in your narrative, you can ask yourself a more general question. Are the responses that you gave a reflection of your typical behavior? Think of several other examples of loneliness and determine if your answers are the same or not. We do tend to battle to participate in habitual ways.

### Allied Conditions

Discussion of loneliness can expand its meaning beyond usefulness. Loneliness is not the only suffering we endure, and it is hardly the worst. To consider it as a catchall for all our negative experience not only overemphasizes but obscures its nature. Also, we usually experience it in association with other conditions: isolation, alienation, depression, and grief. Comparison with these conditions will clarify for us what loneliness is and is not.

We know that loneliness and isolation are not identical. We have been alone and not lonely, and we have been in the midst of others, yet lonely. However, we still tend to assume too quickly that the isolated are lonely. There are many successful styles of life, including those oriented around couplehood, work, extended family, the community at large, or around the self in relative isolation.[13] Despite our biases, it would be difficult to prove that any one of these styles is more conducive or less conducive to loneliness. Moreover, the occasion for loneliness is affected by these styles. The death of a spouse will not cause us so much loneliness if we are oriented more toward work than toward couplehood. Even those of us who hate our work may find our community involvement by means of it, and become lonely upon retirement. So it is useful for us to move beyond the bias that isolation necessarily produces loneliness and to determine what kind of isolation affects us in what ways.

Another condition often related to loneliness, and sometimes confused with it, is alienation. What is alien is foreign and wholly different. To be estranged is to be detached and broken off from others or from oneself. We feel not just isolated but "out of it." But this is not identical to loneliness. Impersonal work conditions may lead us to alienation from others, and then, in turn, to loneliness. And when we are lonely we may become alien to ourselves if we hide from the loneliness, or alienated from others if we try to manipulate them in order to remove our loneliness. But we can be lonely and not estranged. Separation of a couple can be the consequence of a death as well as of a divorce. In the latter, we will probably be both lonely and alienated, while in the former, estrangement may be relatively absent. Or we can experience both conditions together, each one contributing to the other. When we are partially alienated, we are likely to be lonely, and vice versa. Either one can be first in setting up this vicious circle.

We must also beware the danger of equating loneliness and depression. Both conditions give rise to feelings of sadness, anger, guilt, worthlessness, and helplessness.[14] We focus so much on depression in our lives that we may miss those occasions when the symptoms really indicate loneliness. Perhaps it is easier to confess the one than the other. But they are not identical. We can be depressed about matters other than separation, and we can be lonely without being greatly angry or guilty or worthless. Yet depression is a likely consequence, for loneliness is the "sweet sorrow" that comes from parting. Anger at self or other is common in loneliness. And our mood can develop overwhelmingly and expose the sense of helplessness which turns sweetness bitter. It is most important to understand, however, that total helplessness is not involved in loneliness, for this would mean abandonment of the search. We may feel ourselves to be helpless in loneliness, but we are not actually so, our cry of despair being a cry for help based on our faith in its possibility.

The last distinction to make is between loneliness and grief. Grief also gives rise to feelings of sadness, anger, guilt, worthlessness, and helplessness. These symptoms are consequences of a loss. Grief is the process of moving from shock and an inability to surrender the past, into deep distress over the reality of the loss, and then into an integration of what is valuable from the past into a new, meaningful pattern of relationship.[15] Certainly loneliness can be involved in our grieving. But we know that the amount of it will differ. For a woman whose life centered about her husband and who had very little involvement with children, friends, or community, loneliness is likely to be a major aspect of grief when her husband dies. At the other extreme, a husband whose focus is on his work and on community service will have less loneliness on the death of his wife, both because his relationship to his wife was minimal intimacy and because his other relationships continue to sustain him. This is not to say he will grieve less, but only that loneliness will not be as important as such other responses as hostility and guilt. In addition, we should note that whereas our loneliness is about loss of relationship, grief can pertain to other kinds of losses, such as physical health and stages of life cycle. Finally, we can recall the discovery of Frankie in *The Member of the Wedding* that possibility of relationship fosters loneliness. Grief over loss is not involved. The two conditions go together easily but not necessarily.

Before you reach the end of this chapter, it is appropriate to consider these allied conditions in your own life. Refer once more to your loneliness narrative, and answer the following questions briefly and concretely.

1. To what extent and in what way was isolation involved?
2. To what extent and in what way was alienation involved?
3. To what extent and in what way was depression involved?
4. To what extent and in what way was grief involved?
5. In what ways are the presence of these allied conditions in your loneliness narrative typical in your loneliness experiences?
6. Recall one or more occasions on which your awareness of the allied conditions concealed from you the more fundamental presence of loneliness.
7. Recall one or more occasions on which your awareness of loneliness concealed from you the more fundamental presence of the allied conditions.

*Conclusion*

Our attempt to see and understand loneliness is likely to inflate it beyond reason. However, we do need to be related to our environment in order to survive and we have the awareness of this need as a tool for our use. Loneliness, then, is not an incidental aspect, but an essential part of being human. Still, the danger remains of separating loneliness from other states entirely. More dangerous is the assumption that loneliness takes priority over all other states at all times. We may risk our lives out of loneliness sometimes, but other times we will risk loneliness in order to eat and sleep. Loneliness may enable us to move toward another human being in spite of anxiety, but not always, for we will often endure separation in order to feel and be safe with our habitual self-esteem. So loneliness is not a driving force that knows no obstacle and rides roughshod over every other human situation. Our flexibility and creativity guarantee that loneliness can be harnessed, directed, subdued, or even nearly extinguished. For some of us, loneliness can become the most significant condition. For others of us, it may never be so. The mood of loneliness in us tends to overemphasize its power. So also does our self-pity. Our understanding of what loneliness is should help us resist such temptation.

# CHAPTER III

# *Why We Are Lonely*

When we are lonely, we cry out, "Why me?" This is a protest about being forsaken. It is also a question about cause. Both of these questions prompt reflection which can deepen our understanding of relationship and of the nature of our participation in it. So we explore the four causes of loneliness.

### The Separate Self

The first and deepest cause of loneliness is the human condition itself. We are born to be lonely.[16] We are separate selves and know it. This is not just recognition of individual differences. Even as identical twins, we experience our selves as separate. No matter how strongly related two people are, they remain two rather than one. Two lifelong companions experience dying separately with full awareness that only one dies while the other lives and that this gulf is not totally bridged. Indeed, it is the very strength of the relationship that makes the gulf so apparent. Nor when two lovers witness a sunset together or two parents witness the achievement of a child is the enjoyment of that of one rather than of two. Even in the most companionable moments, there is separateness. Again, the more companionable the moment, the more awareness of separateness at the same time. Why are we lonely? Because we are both separate from each other and participants in each other. To be both, and to know we are both, is to be lonely.

There is no return or advance to a time and place of no loneliness.

But we are not above trying. To know ourselves only as separate individuals, to be totally unaware of the possibilities of participation and community, is to be without loneliness. To know ourselves only as members of community, to be totally unaware of ourselves as individuals, is to be without loneliness. With either kind of flight, we are attempting escape from our humanity. Loneliness is caused by the human condition.

This awareness of our condition is not something we are inclined to seek out or maintain in attention. Even when experienced during a peak moment of a relationship, it is awesome. And we are closer to terror when we have such awareness in the absence of relationship. The mood of loneliness is not entirely wrong, as it unleashes our sense of fragility in relationship. So our experience of such basic loneliness is rare. In protecting ourselves from it we may even have the defensive belief that loneliness is unnecessary and avoidable. The human condition is otherwise. We may exist at times outside loneliness, but we are never beyond it.

### Changes in Relationship

The second-level cause of loneliness is what normally comes to mind. The focus is on a person or object that has been lost. We add to this the understanding that loneliness occurs also over what has not yet been gained: discovery of a potential for relationship. These constitute the cause of loneliness due to changes in relationship. We understand these changes to be inevitable. Even if accidental, they are well within the order of things. Our average expectable environment includes friends who move to another part of the country, toys that break, and even death due to the collision of cars. All these are environmental inevitabilities. We even say, after a falling out of relationship, "Ah, well, people change."

Note that the first and second levels of cause do differ. Both reflect the human condition, but the first is about the permanent situation of being both individual and participant, while the second involves change as occasional and not continual. The latter can be overcome. Changes that cause loneliness can also offer possibilities of new relationships or prompt search of them. We do make new friends, buy new cars, adopt children. This is not to claim that all loneliness from this cause can be overcome. When a couple have been together for fifty or more years, the death of one most likely leaves a permanent loneliness regardless of what new relationships occur. And when we realize that a certain kind of relationship, however much desired, will probably always be beyond our grasp, then our loneliness will remain with us. But we should not assume that changes in relationship necessarily and inevitably leave permanent loneliness. This would be a defensive reaction, protecting us from exploring possibilities that are natural and expectable.

### Problems in Self and Society

In moving to the third level of cause, we consider what is neither fundamental nor accidental but is exceedingly common. There are individual and group traits which foster loneliness. Some adults appear to be loneliness prone. These may be persons whose relationships are uncertain, unclear, and hesitant. We who are this way are most powerfully affected by changes in relationship. Further, we are likely to be seeking relationship continually and yet maintaining all specific relationships in a state of flux. The need for security forbids clear commitment and requires continual testing. Others of us are shy, distant, wistful outsiders who long to dive into the communal swim and either do not know how or have been held back by some restraining forces. And still others of us may be not only uncertain or shy but also strange to others. In these cases, our problems began very early in life within the family, when we concluded that our need for tenderness was futile or dangerous. By the time we came into full contact with others of our age, our behavior may have become more related to fantasy than to social reality and sufficiently odd so that they laughed, punished, and abandoned us. A shy or uncertain person who is relatively "normal" can attract other shy or uncertain people at least. The strange one who is either outgoing or certain of relationships can move into a connection. But we who are both strange and shy or uncertain are nearly helpless persons from whom others keep their distance. Whether uncertain, shy, strange, or any combination of these, we are prone to loneliness.

As just stated, such proneness does not happen to an individual in a vacuum. Families foster loneliness in their children when they ignore them, overprotect them, or give them mixed signals on how to behave. But families without such inner difficulties can also experience loneliness because they are living according to the dictates of their society. Groups vary in the amount of change in relationship caused by assorted customs. For example, the high degree of mobility in American culture probably fosters loneliness. There is physical mobility: movement from one residence to another as the adults change jobs; reliance on special clinics for medical care that exist outside one's own neighborhood; increasing use of retirement homes and nursing homes for the elderly and sick. There is also social mobility: movement up the ladder in an organization involves leaving old friendships and forming new ones, and movement from one class to another involves far greater changes. Another kind of mobility is in the realm of values. For example, a male executive used to do what he was told when asked to change residence. Nowadays, he and his wife can have their own second thoughts. These new options generate uncertainty and tentativeness. Or customs can change in sexual behavior. However beneficial those customs have been in the long run, couples can find the old patterns of relating becoming tentative. When such value changes occur, we are likely to experience uncertainty, less support from others involved, and increased loneliness. And when such change is directly related to interpersonal matters, the loneliness will be marked. Mobility in our society has many benefits, and I doubt we would want it decreased, but we should note that the physical, social, and value changes do foster loneliness.

This consideration of problems in self and society should not let us forget that loneliness per se is not destructive any more than its causes are necessarily destructive. A little uncertainty, shyness, and individuality can be harmless and even creative. Mobility in society can be the same. And loneliness itself is a creative condition in general. The issue is one of degree. Too much of one of these characteristics in the individual or the society can lead to severe problems in relationships. Too little can lead to stagnation at immature levels of relationship. As for loneliness: "A little, please, perhaps just a little more than we want, but not too much more." This is a reasonable and healthy request. And we should remember that the responsibility for problematic loneliness usually is related to both the society and the individual. What is unfortunate is not just that society can work against us, but that it is we and society who work against ourselves in fostering more loneliness than we can handle creatively.

*Increasing Loneliness*

The fourth-level cause of loneliness is the most superficial, yet a source of great and unnecessary suffering. We who are already lonely find loneliness increased by the responses of others and by our own responses as well. This exacerbation is usually caused by responses based on flight from, and protection against, loneliness rather than on acceptance, understanding, and movement toward companionship.

Loneliness is a condition that does not always call attention to itself. Other persons tend to be less aware of our loneliness than we are. By contrast, they may be more aware of our anger than we are, and more concerned to do something about it, especially to protect themselves. Anger, sadness, and joy seem to bid for response, especially because of the accompanying shouting, crying, or laughing. But loneliness appears neither welcoming nor coercive to others. This can be a reason why society pays little attention to the lonely. When the loneliness of another is perceived, we can either flee or fight. On the one hand, we can simply remove ourselves physically or psychologically. What we do with lonely people is to leave them alone. If we do not leave physically, we take flight by ignoring the loneliness itself. Surely you can recall occasions when you have done so. We do this in order not to see it in ourselves. On the other hand, we can stand and attack. Two kinds of fighting occur. One approach is to counterattack by belittling loneliness. This is an attempt to encourage by arguing that the loneliness is not so large as is believed—will not last long, is not serious, or applies only to a certain realm and not to all others. We try to put loneliness into a very small perspective. At the most ludicrous, we counsel a bereaved spouse: "Don't worry, you'll get married again soon." The other kind of fight is encouragement of relationship. We try to get the person into couplings or groupings, forcing new relationships. These attacks on loneliness are not entirely negative, but are made without understanding or tolerance of loneliness. We know that we have made these attacks also. Yet separation and loneliness must be embraced before they can be overcome.

With or without such exacerbation of our loneliness by society, we are likely to contribute to the problem ourselves. It is in this response to our own loneliness that we see occurrence of a vicious circle. To paraphrase a saying: "We have nothing to fear about loneliness but our fear of it." When the fear is too great, we try to renounce relationship per se to some degree. This partial renunciation sustains and can increase loneliness. Self-deception enters and hides both our fear of loneliness and our despair. The contribution we make is pervasive and varied. Here is a list of some of our common maneuvers.[17] You should be able to see yourself in some of them, and think of others that I have missed.

We claim that only one specific person could ever be the right one for us. Then, after unrequited love, no intimacy is possible again.

We can attempt relationship with the unattainable. We select someone as the object of a possible relationship with clear knowledge that he or she is not attracted to us and will reject us. Or we can be a nurse who falls in love with a dying patient, or a young man who falls in love with an older, married woman who will not leave her husband. By these means we can claim that we are trying to relate.

We can be attracted to people in general, participating with them in limited ways. Those of us who are like this can work well in organizations founded for the welfare of the human race, functioning as clergy, nurses, teachers, and other providers of human services— these allowing relatively safe, one-way relationships.

We can acknowledge our renunciation, priding ourselves on giving up love in the name of duty to God, the party, our country, fellow human beings, creativity, or whatever. This parades both our suffering and our nobility.

We can continually fuss about our relationships. Such churning without reflection leads us nowhere, bores our partners, and abuses the relationship. We are quite preoccupied, but in such a way that others are put off and kept off to our concealed satisfaction. Those of us who do dramatize our loneliness, who turn this very shy condition into a public spectacle, do not abate it but increase it.

Finally, there is the opposite to the above, those who eliminate all fuss with talk of realism and discarding of romance. There is a lowering of expectations and an increase of distance and disengagement. This may be described as "cool sex" or "new intimacy." We decide not to be vulnerable and that wounds are out of order. Yet, as has been said, "To love is to be lonely."[18]

These are some of the ways we use to deceive ourselves and increase our loneliness. If you did not see yourself described at all, read them over again. However, this focus on our own contribution should not eclipse the contribution of others to our increased loneliness. Flight and fight by others and by ourselves is what so spoils the creative side of loneliness.

## Conclusion

We conclude by referring back to our experiences of loneliness in an attempt to recognize why we were lonely. It is not easy to do so, and we cannot be certain that we are correct in our analysis. But this attempt to understand our causes may still engender some discoveries about ourselves and our relationships. Allow at least fifteen minutes for your reflecting.

1. Recall your written narrative of a loneliness experience. What do you think was the leading cause?
2. What other causes, if any, were involved? In what ways?
3. Recall three other loneliness experiences, each of which has one of the other causes as predominant.
4. What are the problems in society that foster loneliness in you the most? In your family. In your community. In your national society.
5. What are the problems in yourself that foster loneliness in you the most?
6. What are the ways in which others have increased your loneliness?
7. What are the ways in which you have increased your loneliness?
8. Which of the above questions are the most difficult to answer? Why?

I hope this outline of four causes and our attempt to connect them with our experiences of loneliness have achieved three things. First, it should help us to avoid too simple an approach to the analysis of our experience. The danger lies in stressing only one cause. To dwell only on the separate self is to avoid the role played by our own personality and society in fostering unnecessary loneliness. And it is also to dilute the sharp experience of loneliness due to change in relationship by death which can severely trouble the contented philosopher who focuses on the human condition. But those who dwell only on the unnecessary causes of loneliness can be tempted to try to abolish all loneliness, to attempt futilely to overcome it once and for all. So, using the four causes reminds us that the sources of loneliness vary and that there is the dual danger of either denying loneliness or despairing over it. We can and must struggle to participate even though the challenge is unending.

Second, these reasons why we are lonely are levels of depth and degrees of necessity. They constitute a scale that can be a guide for our analysis of each loneliness experience. For example, when a spouse dies, there is the possibility of increasing self-knowledge by recognizing that loneliness is a basic aspect of being human. Also, one's own reactions to the loneliness of the death can increase that self-knowledge. Focus on the change due to death is not sufficient. These causes lie on a continuum that should be traveled as fully as possible if loneliness is to be fully explored. It may be that the most pertinent level is the one typically overlooked by the lonely person. If our exploration of the causes is thorough, there should be some surprises, and therefore some education about the self, the other, and the relationship. So, were you surprised at any point while you reflected on your response to the questions or during the course of reading this chapter? I hope you were, and it is likely that this occurred because you were moved along the continuum. If no surprises occurred at all, you might review the questions and answers.

Finally, our response to these causes should remind us of the richness of our loneliness experiences. To discover ourselves to be lonely for more than one reason, and for different reasons on different occasions, is to see our own complexity and variety. We should tolerate it and, if and when we can, enjoy it. Why are we lonely? Our answers reveal us to be interesting people.

# CHAPTER IV

# *Realms of Relationship*

Thus far, our exploration of relationship and loneliness has been about loved ones—our intimate connection with spouse, lover, close friend, or member of the family. This relationship with a loved one is only one of five kinds, the others being groups of people, generations, things, and the world. Because we can relate in all these vast areas, the ways in which we experience loneliness and companionship are innumerable and varied indeed. The purpose of this chapter is to remind us of all the possibilities of relationship. This includes, of course, all the ways in which we have been and can be lonely.

## Individuals and Groups

The first two realms of relationship are the most recognized and will be discussed together. We experience loneliness and companionship with both an individual and a group of people. In both forms of loneliness, we have a driving restlessness and a yearning search for relationship—separation and search. But the symptoms differ.[19] When we are lonely over the absence of a close attachment to an individual, the stress reminds us of a small child who fears abandonment by the mother. We are tense, apprehensive, and vigilant. Absence is a powerful presence. Our world appears desolate and barren, and we appear to ourselves as empty and hollow. This happens to us as small children who have lost a mother and as adults who have lost a loved one. The symptoms of group loneliness are different. Our reactions are like those of an older child whose friends are away. We are bored and aimless, feeling ourselves on the margin of real life. Concerning these two realms of relationship and the experience of loneliness in them, there are three likely surprises. We are shocked when life's events remind us of the obvious.

The first surprise is our discovery of the depth of our attachments to individuals. For example, we assume depth in our relationships to those we love, but forget about its existence when the connection is less than ideal. Some of us are still firmly attached to our parents, even though we may not wish to be in some ways. How surprised we may be by loneliness after a divorce. Here we are, finally free of an undesired, crippling relationship, not really very ambivalent about "splitting," and really geared up to begin a new life—and then we are overwhelmed by loneliness. Our depth of attachment to some people can surprise us.

A second surprise occurs when we discover that our group loneliness can be equally deep. We tend to play down this loneliness, but we can find it more of a threat than the individual kind, especially at certain stages in our lives. As adolescents we were all too aware of feeling "left out" or "on the sidelines." Seeing ourselves or believing that others see us as wallflowers is very painful. The old and dying may be abandoned, and this loss may contribute to their death by hastening it. In a study of older people who died in hospitals without apparent cause, it was found that group loneliness was pervasive.[20] And the social network is important throughout our lives. Mobility threatens it. Social networks are lost by children of upwardly mobile parents and by the elderly who are placed in homes. What happens to us when we are middle-aged? When a family moves to a new community, the working husband integrates quickly and easily into the social network of his job. The woman at home is not integrated into the new network at all. She has neither place nor function in her new community. She is lonely. She may not be aware of it. If she is, she may feel guilty. If she does not feel guilty and mentions her confusing pain to her husband, he may innocently reply, "But you have me, dear." He is sustained by the social network and does not know it. She is not sustained and may not know it. Recent changes in our family work patterns will change this particular loneliness. The point is that our need and efforts to be accepted into, and maintained in, a social network are fundamental and pervasive. Recall a time in a group when you felt ignored, barely tolerated, or despised. And recall the personal chaos this caused. Because we forget, discovery of the depth of our attachment can surprise us.

The third surprise may occur when we discover that individual and group loneliness pertain to different realms of relationship and need to be resolved differently. The remedy for óne is not the remedy for the other. The death of a spouse causes group loneliness as well as individual loneliness. A widow has to function as a single person, and her new social role will not fit easily into the familiar social network. She is likely to become quite marginal to it, especially if the death occurs during the middle years, before widowhood is common among her peers. The first aspect of the surprise is that the end of one kind of relationship causes rupture in the other kind. The second aspect is that the solution to the one will not suffice for the other. The widow may seek and find a new social network, but it will not fill the gap left by the spouse. We often counsel ourselves and others to keep busy and become more involved. These are valuable enterprises which will help counter group loneliness, removing boredom and meaningless routine, but then a severe letdown can occur when it is realized that the inner emptiness still remains. The two realms of relationship affect each other but remain distinct. We know this in our heads, but our grieving hearts can be surprised.

*Generations*

The realm of the generations begins with our family and extends to history and to the human race as a whole. Because we can recall the past and anticipate the future, our social life has extraordinary breadth. Through our dependence as young children on our parents and as old parents on our middle-aged children, we are given the possibility of becoming aware of the generations immediately before and after our own. To discover these and more distant possibilities is to experience the separation and search of loneliness, and failure to seize these possibilities involves a diminution of our humanity. It is likely that the breadth of our loneliness in the social realm is far too narrow, for we attend mostly to the present generation in our friends and lovers. From whom have we come and toward whom are we going? We remain lonely, or less than lonely, until we find our beginnings and endings.

We begin our awareness of the past generations through our families and extended families. The question, "Where did I come from?"

is not just about sex, but is asking a parent or grandparent: "Where do you come from?" and "What was it like when you were my age?" Juvenile and preadolescent children can be quite amazed at the new mystery of generations. Then, the middle years provide renewed interest as grandparents die, parents become dependent upon their adult children, and the younger children grow up and begin to leave. And then, perhaps, the very old who are close to death and connected with grandchildren and great-grandchildren may be prompted to explore the generations one last time. The generations become important in times of transition. To move somewhere, we have to know where we have been.

As we develop the need to relate to the generations within the family, so also do we develop our relationship to the society of the past. The child receives oral tradition about earlier times in the lives of parents and grandparents. Later, we are exposed to academic disciplines for history, but popular culture remains our greater source. We are connected with the past by means of lore: such heroes as Lincoln, Martin Luther King, Jr., Napoleon, Jesus; such events as the Civil War, the parting of the Red Sea, the first space flight; and such objects as the American flag, Latin words in a Catholic Mass, and Egyptian pyramids. Historical novels, nostalgic cinema, clothing fashions of an earlier period—preoccupation with the life of past generations is marked. We should not study the past in order to repeat it as primitives did, or not to repeat it, as many moderns do, but simply to become connected with it, to relate to the past as a companion. Such a connection allows us to travel into the future.

The future can also be a companion without which we are lonely. Our ability to anticipate is a key source for survival. Much of this work is mundane, but not all. Those ancient theologians who speculated in great detail about our future in heaven are matched by contemporary "theologians" who speculate in science fact and fiction about the future in this or other worlds. The futures we envision become companions with which we converse. To wonder about what might be is work for survival, because we can enter the future best when it is our companion. The challenge is to discover a future that is not entirely ours. As children can begin to see the past by means of their parents, we can begin to see the future by means of our children. When they are no longer mere extensions of us, their future becomes seen as different from our own. Only then is it a companion. A leap from the future of our own present to the future of someone else's present enlarges our future considerably. Our own future will come to an end, but the future of another may continue further. If the link to the future of another is made, the loneliness of coming to an end in death is diminished. So also is the loneliness of being superseded by the young or of having lived beyond our own time diminished. To actually have a future is to have a future that is not entirely our own.

Generational loneliness is all too common, although not commonly recognized. Youth experience it. They feel cut off from the past and from the middle-aged generation which represents it. This robs them of a sense of the future as well. The old know about this also. They have little future left to welcome and so turn to others who represent it for them—the young and the middle-aged. But these relationships do not always work and so they feel they have lived beyond their times. They finally become uncertain about their past as well. Those of us in our middle years may feel disconnected from the generations on both sides. All such loneliness is inevitable and valuable, unless it becomes chronic. Without connection to the generations, there is no care. Without care, there is no survival. Our loneliness occurs to prompt us to join up with the human race. Most of us, I suspect, could stand a little more generational loneliness rather than less. We do not always know when we are unaware of our beginnings and endings. To know them is to know the story of humanity, and to know that story is to know ourselves as part of it.

### Things

The fourth realm of relationship consists of all our companions that are not people—both the natural and the artificial objects in our lives. This nonhuman environment is extensive and important. We depend on it for food and shelter and for stimulation of our senses of seeing, hearing, tasting, smelling, and touching. Given these needs for survival and stimulation, it is no surprise that we become quite attached to a variety of things.

The very young child develops a sense of the overall space in which she lives and of the important objects in it. She may have a room that is hers, a special place in the room that belongs to her most of all—such as her bed or play corner—and a group of toys that are especially meaningful. The child's object world is a companion—really, a number of companions. And if she is required to move into another environment, she will do her best to take her companions with her. Without the familiar, she becomes lonely. We adults are the same. Indeed, we have taken these early things with us in memory. We can go home again by recollecting our room and toys, our neighborhood space with its special places for play. Try this and you will be surprised by the wealth of detail you can recall. The things were companions for us.

It is difficult to be both concrete and meaningful about the present things to which we are attached because they vary enormously. The list is unending: house or apartment, cars, clothing, furniture, indoor plants, outdoor trees and streams, city buildings, books, jewelry, tools for shop or kitchen, and pets. What do you possess that replaces the child's blanket or teddy bear? What toy do you relate to? When you move your living quarters, what items do you install first? When you travel, are there unnecessary things that accompany you away from home? And what things do you refuse to throw away? Some of our closest companions in the object world are junk. We may see and fondle these little bits rarely, but are unhappy when they are lost. We even pass them on to the next generation, caring more for them than do those who have to receive them. And wouldn't we feel sorry for people who had no junk of their own?

We may fail to see that we have such material companions. This can happen because our objects differ from those of children and of earlier peoples. The toys of children are limited because access is somewhat controlled by adults, whereas our own toys vary greatly. Earlier peoples treated objects with utmost respect, especially natural objects. We may also find occasion to relate to nature in our delight with wind, sand, and star. To spend a morning watching birds feed their young, a day traveling beside a mountain stream, or a week climbing a mountain is to find companions. But we are not so dependent on our natural environment and may miss seeing our similarity to earlier peoples because we relate more to artificial things.

If we do see ourselves as having object companions, we are likely to disparage such relationships. We do this in two ways. On the one hand, we refer to materialism and conspicuous waste, and preach that adults should be less attached to things. Of course, this attitude is contradicted by our desire to preserve old buildings that are no longer of use, create objects that are desired only as decorations, and stare at, fondle, and kneel before pictures, statues, crosses, and stars connected with our religions. Those who see our material companions negatively are very likely seeing only some objects used by others as companions and remaining quite unaware of their own material friends. On the other hand, we can disparage our attachments by assuming that they occur because of deprivation and are not really companionships anyway. It is assumed that those of us who love animals or plants are either unwilling or unable to love humans. Further, it is thought that this is a response to loss of relationship with humans and can be tolerated under these circumstances, especially in children, old people who live alone, and the recently bereaved. In addition, it is claimed that these objects are not real companions, but only extensions of ourselves. Flowers and cats do not interact with us as fully as do humans, and we are attracted to them precisely because of this, because we can do with them as we please, according to our own fantasies. This is a demeaning reaction based on the occurrence of abuse. We do select things as substitutes and project our fantasies onto them. But we can do otherwise. We relate to things just because they are there and are of interest to us in their own right as people are, and not just because we are deprived of some other kind of relationship. Material objects have a life of their own that can intersect with ours if we allow it to. The fact that some of us cannot relate to people should not obscure the fact that some of us cannot relate to the nonhuman beings of this world.

So object loneliness occurs. There is homesickness, scene-sickness, toy-sickness, and so on. Some of us may be lonely because we are separated from and are searching for the green grass that was so close to us as rural and semirural children and is so far from us as urban adults. Vacations may be partly a response to this loneliness. But what else have we lost for which we continually seek? What have we not lost, and yet are unaware of possessing, that is meaningful to us? What objects have we never had a relationship to and yet seek out? What new thing companions might we enjoy? Are we really less thing deprived than people deprived?

*World*

The fifth and last realm of relationship is that of existence as a whole where the world is companion and the loneliness is world loneliness. We want to respond to life with both wonder and welcome. We want to be astonished and yet be at home.[21] Companionship with various parts is not sufficient. Is our world against us or indifferent to us? If we conclude that it lacks goodwill, we become "strangers in a strange land," pilgrims in search of the world as companion.

Religion is the traditional institution whose primary purpose is to call attention to our disconnection, and then to establish, maintain, and renew our relationship with the world. We do have a sense that our religious heroes are the most lonely of human beings: Luther making his stand, Moses knowing that he would not enter the Promised Land, and Jesus having no place to lay his head. For some, the ultimate loneliness is symbolized by the cry of Jesus: "Why hast thou forsaken me?" The Christian celebration of world loneliness occurs once a year on Good Friday. For earlier peoples, it often occurred when the sun provided the shortest day. God is the ultimate symbol of the world as companion, and the ultimate loneliness is, therefore, the absence of God. For this symbol to lose its power and/or meaning is a catastrophe. Jesus, and some gifted others who experience it, recover and bring back to us new revelations about relationship with the world. Out of this comes the body of myth and ritual which remind us that the world is our home. Myth is our affirmation of the world as companion, and ritual is our participation in this friendly world. Divination, healing, and other special functions of the traditional clergy and their institutions are essentially reminders of world relationship.

Most of us are not concerned most of the time about world loneliness and companionship. Indeed, we may assume that we are never concerned, that the issue has been outgrown. But modern versions of the concern are profuse, however invisible. It appears in the growing interest in Oriental philosophy and religion, in the widespread addiction to the occult, in humanistic psychology, and even in some discussions of theoretical physics. Individually, we can become successful in companionships in other realms and still find ourselves lacking something. Or we can become so lonely in another realm that it spreads to the totality of existence. In either case, we can be pushed and shoved into a discovery of the whole. Then we wonder what it is all about, why things are as they are, and how we are to live accordingly.

This discovery of the whole is frequently a recognition of two worlds. The profane world is exceedingly fragile, with the companionship risky and the loneliness overwhelming. The sacred world is one of relationship per se, the source of that companionship which occurs in the profane. This other world may be totally apart from the daily one, as in the afterlife of classical Christianity, a historically located next world as in Judaism, or in the midst of the present world, as in a variety of mystical traditions. Knowledge of these two worlds presents the temptation to live in only the sacred one. This perversion of ignoring the parts of the world—all the other realms of relationship—is different from the valid discovery of the sacred that both recognizes and supports other relationships. Our discovery of the world as a whole is what grants us the courage to be lonely and to continue the search for relationship to the parts of the world. Indeed, it may prompt us to awareness of possibilities we have not realized before.

Coming face-to-face with the ultimate Companion is awesome and demanding. Facing solutions requires more courage than facing problems. But in this case it is the solution that grants the courage. Companionship with the world is the affirmation of the possibility of relationships in all other realms. Our traditional religious myth and ritual assist us in this coming face-to-face. If we are without a living tradition of this sort, it is likely that we have developed, however rudimentarily, our own individual traditions. These should be acknowledged, affirmed, and developed.

Before we go further into discussion of these realms, it is time to be sure we can see our own loneliness in each of them. Take twenty minutes to recall and note in writing some appropriate experiences. We will be using them again shortly and later on.

1. Note briefly two experiences of loneliness in the realm of individual relationship.
2. Note briefly two experiences of loneliness in the realm of group relationship.
3. Note briefly two experiences of loneliness in the realm of the generations.
4. Note briefly two experiences of loneliness in the realm of artificial objects.
5. Note briefly two experiences of loneliness in the realm of nature and natural objects.
6. Note briefly two experiences of loneliness in the realm of the world as a whole.
7. In which of the five realms is it easiest to find examples of loneliness? Why?

8. In which of the five realms is it most difficult to find examples of loneliness? Why?

This exercise takes considerable time, but it gives us much material to explore over and over again. For our present purposes, it is enough to be reminded of our connections in all five realms of relationship and of our loneliness in them. Further, we may be prompted into becoming more aware of those realms we understand the least and/or are least conscious of.

## Conclusion

The purpose of this chapter has been to remind us of all the possibilities for relationship and for loneliness. Three final observations help to emphasize this.

The first point is that the different kinds of loneliness are likely to occur together. Consider again the death of a spouse. Individual loneliness is involved, of course. So also is group loneliness, because the social network is likely to be disturbed. The presence of the other realms is not so obvious. Yet we know that the meaning of the past and the future changes when a death occurs. A planned trip to Europe is not the same, nor are relationships to children and to grandparents. Our pasts and futures have to be redefined and new relationships established. Object loneliness is normal. When a loved one dies, we are severed from one who is an art object, a teddy bear or a blanket, and simply a part of the world that is enjoyable and comforting to touch, smell, taste, hear, and see. And there can be world loneliness also. Any part can symbolize the whole. For this purpose we usually take care to rely on parts that do not easily and frequently become separated from us—stars in the heavens and the spring that returns each year. The great daring of Christianity in selecting a human being to symbolize the whole world as Companion could not suffice without the equally daring dogma of his resurrection. Spouses may be such a symbol also. This symbol breaks down when death occurs, so we have hopes of immortality and reunion with the departed. It is possible that the death of a spouse can involve any and all of the five realms of relationship. And this could be true of any other event, such as a change of residence or the loss of a pet. Our loneliness is far richer than we realize.

The second point is about the distinctiveness of each realm and the inability of one to substitute adequately for another. Our separation within a realm should involve a search within that realm, and loneliness within a realm is resolved only by a new relationship within it. However, since any experience of loneliness may involve disconnection from more than one realm, it can be appropriate for us to search for a relationship that is not immediately sensible to ourselves or others. If a man who loses a wife purchases a pet dog, he may not just be searching for a substitute for an individual relationship, but primarily replacing the material object that his wife was. Further, it can be that he is, quite naturally, searching for the most appropriate object and that his selection of the realm reveals the nature of his loss —the realm from which he feels most separated. Such an assumption may help us discover the specifics of the loneliness we experience. There may be attempts at substitution of one realm for another, but it is just as likely that our behavior illustrates the realm in which loneliness is experienced most severely.

Finally, we may note that because the worlds of relationship are discrete and yet overlap, the fact of loneliness prompts us to discover new possibilities. That a material thing cannot replace a human being is a harsh discovery for those who would be inclined to seek and accept such substitution. But we can also discover the satisfaction of relating to a thing in its own right, broadening our experience, understanding, and gratification. To lose a member of our family and then become concerned about the generations does not replace the individual relationship that has been lost, but it does open us to another realm that can serve us well. Loneliness is about possibility. To appreciate only one realm and become separate from a member of it is quite different from knowing all five realms and becoming separated from a member of one of them. The separation is not ended necessarily, but it is put in its place when we are fully aware of and living in all five realms. The unbearable and impossible are made tragic and comprehensible. Our loneliness is richer than we know, and, even so, needs to become richer than it is.

Now we have further questions for you to ask yourselves about your loneliness experiences. Your recollection has to be accompanied by analysis.

1. Recall your written narrative of a loneliness experience. What do you think was the leading realm involved?
2. What other realms, if any, were involved? In what ways?

3. Select any three of the other loneliness experiences you noted down previously. List the realms involved in each one.
4. Out of all these loneliness experiences, select one example where you might have been substituting one realm for another.
5. Out of all these loneliness experiences, select one example where apparent substitution was really a revelation of the nature of the loss, however strange it might have appeared to you or others.
6. Out of all these loneliness experiences, select one example where loneliness in one realm opened you up to possibilities of relationship in another realm.

No doubt you have done enough reflection on your own loneliness for a while. But we should conclude by reminding ourselves about the complexity involved which is due to the combinations of the five realms of relationship with the four causes of loneliness discussed in the previous chapter. First, we need to note that loneliness in any of the five realms can be at any one of the four levels of cause. Typically, we ignore this possibility and limit certain kinds of loneliness to certain causes. So we assume that loneliness over existence as a whole is automatically related to the first-level cause of perceiving the basic human condition of separateness. However, we can be amused and kindly suspicious with some justification about the adolescent philosopher who expresses wonder and awe about the totality of his existence and ignores his troubled shyness. We should be as open with the older adult, paying attention to the possibilities of third- and fourth-level problems in self and society, seeking out the unnecessary causes of world loneliness. The point is that any cause can be related to any realm, and any part of any realm to any cause.

Having made this point, we also remind ourselves that any number of both realms and causes can be participants in a specific experience of loneliness. Our loneliness with regard to a specific person may have several causes, and our loneliness related to another person may have several other causes. Further, the specific causes related to one realm in an experience may be different from the causes related to another realm in the same experience. In the case of the death of a spouse, loneliness about the loss of a material object may occur mostly at the second level of changes in relationship, while loneliness about the loss of a symbol of the world may occur at the third level of problems in the self. Because of the extensive combinations of realms and causes in a single experience of loneliness, analysis is confusing.

Our theme is that loneliness is a condition rich with variety and complexity. To see and tolerate this is difficult. Yet it is important to do so because such exploration opens possibilities into the conditions of solitude and companionship. Loneliness is about possibilities.

# Solitude

# CHAPTER V

## *What Solitude Is*

Alone. This word gives rise to a sense of great isolation. Our visual images of it are powerful and primary—Robinson Crusoe on his island, Admiral Byrd on the Antarctic ice, Lindbergh in the air, or Chittenden in his tiny sailboat on the high seas. Our typical image of aloneness shows a single human being in the center of a vast and limitless space. The other common image is the urban one of people together and yet not in touch. René Magritte shows the head of a man and of a woman about to kiss, but their heads are covered by cloth bags. George Tooker shows individuals in the subway, lurking about in isolation, staring with fear at each other, while Edvard Munch shows people in a deathbed scene with their backs turned to one another. With nature or with people, these images suggest the extreme deprivation of total isolation.

Being alone is rare. When we are away from people, we can be in relationship with the natural world. And rarely are we as away from others as we think. Henry David Thoreau's isolation at Walden Pond involved visiting and being visited by people. He was an avid reader who kept in touch with the generations of writers on art and thought, gave detailed attention to the objects of nature, and attended to the world in his contemplation of meaning. It is difficult to imagine any person less alone. His journal reveals a rich awareness of relationship. Consider your own experiences of isolation. To what extent were you really alone?

But aloneness does occur. There are several ways in which we can be alone but not lonely. Solitude is one of these ways. It is defined as recognition of relationship. Different from loneliness and from other states of being alone but not lonely, solitude is a paradoxical state of being alone and yet not alone.

### Ways of Being Alone but Not Lonely

There is a basic way to be alone without the pains of loneliness and without the joys of solitude. This is to be minimally concerned about relationship. There are three ways to do it. The first way is that of minimum involvement with both the self and the world. The extreme example is that of a highly withdrawn, catatonic schizophrenic who is scarcely aware of self or others.[22] Less drastic examples of reclusiveness are common. When we sunbathe on the sunny beach or read the Sunday newspaper on a rainy afternoon, we are *in absentia* from life, existing in a kind of stupor. Such moments of disengagement from self and world are both pleasurable and beneficial. Less so are the more extended times when some of us alter our consciousness by means of drugs or choose to live in underground steam tunnels or Bowery streets. This is a chronic minimalization of involvement, and loss of hope in relationship has occurred. There is a place in our living for reclusive stupor, but not as a permanent condition. As we shall see, solitude is not like this stopping of the world and self in order to get lost, but a passionate reflection on the world and self as found. It is the finding of relationship, and so, not being asleep, but waking up.

The second way of being alone but not lonely is that of minimum involvement with the world. We are alone in order to be by and with ourselves only. Interest and reflection are not eliminated, but are focused on one pole of relationship. This self-interest is legitimate pleasure and useful for us if it is not a chronic substitute for relationship. Chronic individualism is typified by the idiosyncratic people who are highly visible because they stand out against the community. Perhaps we are like this at times, but we are more likely less dramatic in our aloneness. Some of us go about our business of doing our own thing very quietly, causing little fuss. We are loath to examine this peaceful self-absorption critically because of our high valuation of privacy and freedom. But these values pertain to relationship and are meaningless in aloneness. As a chronic state, this holding to ourselves occurs when we see that nothing else in the world does. It is when we are most anxious that we cry out for the self. Aloneness with self alone is unhappy divinity through being less than human. Solitude, by contrast, involves interest in both self and world. It is not self-interest, or world interest, but interest in the self-world relationship. Just as solitude is something other than sleep, so it is something other than chronic masturbation.

The third way of being alone but not lonely is that of minimum involvement with the self. We are alone in order to be with and in another. This happens to us when we are absorbed in some task. You sit at your typewriter and write. You are an accountant and attend to your figures. Or you are preparing a complicated menu for a large number of guests. Are you lonely in your aloneness? Not if you are truly engaged. Some of us spend our working hours in the physical presence of others, but most of us—for example, construction workers, shopkeepers, and researchers—do not. The "presence" of other people is mostly physical most of the time on most jobs. Yet we are not lonely because we are engaged, and loneliness is for the unoccupied. Our extroverted society looks kindly upon this minimalization of self by being fully absorbed in the world. Although it appears less selfish and less dangerous to society, it is not. Chronic engagement is flight from the self, a giving up on actual self-world relationship. For example, to move for a limited time and space into a mass demonstration for peace can be helpful for both self and society, but chronic escape into membership in a parade is not. Involvement is not automatically creative, whether we are joining a group for social action or thinking about a theorem in mathematics. Solitude requires engagement with self as well as with world. Just as solitude is something other than sleep or masturbation, so it is something other than chronic busyness.

Now we look at our own experiences of being alone without being lonely. Respond to the following questions briefly and concretely.

1. Recall an experience of aloneness when you were minimally involved with both self and world. How was this aloneness useful?
2. Recall an experience of aloneness when you were minimally involved with the world, focusing on the self. How was this aloneness useful?
3. Recall an experience of aloneness when you were minimally involved with the self, focusing on the world. How was this aloneness useful?

4. Which of these three ways of being alone do you tend to use chronically? What do you gain by this behavior? What do you lose?

*Solitude and Loneliness Compared*

When we do not commit the error of equating solitude with any of the other forms of being alone, then we usually proceed by contrasting it with loneliness. We appreciate solitude because it is three things that loneliness is not—pleasant, free, and timeless.

May Sarton once spent a year of relative aloneness and recorded her reflections in *Journal of a Solitude*.[23] If you give her words time to create a spell, you will find that the following passage evokes the mood of solitude. If someone else is present, read it aloud. If not, read it in a leisurely fashion.

> Today I feel centered and time is a friend instead of the old enemy. It was zero this morning. I have a fire burning in my study, yellow roses and mimosa on my desk. There is an atmosphere of festival, of release, in the house. We are one, the house and I, and I am happy to be alone—time to think, time to be. This kind of open-ended time is the only luxury that really counts and I feel stupendously rich to have it. And for the moment I have a sense of fulfillment both about my life and about my work that I have rarely experienced until this year or perhaps until these last weeks. I look to my left and the transparent blue sky behind a flame-colored cyclamen, lifting about thirty winged flowers to the light, makes an impression of stained glass, light-flooded. I heave the vast heap of unanswered letters into a box at my feet, so I don't see them. And now I am going to make one more try to get that poem right.[24]

Such delight! This is a cozy scene with physical comfort, but much more. She is at ease with her past and her future, and her present is a creative challenge. Her words are those of a cat purring. We can recall such moments ourselves when a flood of joy takes charge of our awareness and no absence is minded. Solitude is being alone with well-being.

Sarton says more than this. She communicates a sense of freedom.

Unanswered mail can be put aside so she can work on her poem. There is freedom from constraints. When lonely, we are not free from people. In solitude, we are quite delighted by not having our loved ones around and do not feel guilty about it either. It is not that we do not love them and enjoy them, but that we need to empty them out of our lives for a while. To not have to answer is a treat whether we are harried parents of young children or bureaucrats frustrated by forms in quadruplicate. But Sarton does want to write a poem. The freedom is for something, not just from something, and often this is for creative work. We really cannot be answerable to others without freedom for leisurely reflection when our accustomed habits of problem-solving are relaxed and novelties can occur. We need the freedom to be surprised. Wordsworth speaks of seeing a host of daffodils dancing in the breeze, and then adds:

> . . . when on my couch I lie
> In vacant or in pensive mood,
> They flash upon that inward eye
> Which is the bliss of solitude;
> And then my heart with pleasure fills,
> And dances with the daffodils.[25]

It is the "inward eye" that brings both pleasure and creative vision. It is no different in the sciences and elsewhere. Solitude is required for the freedom for creativity.

Finally, we have a sense of timelessness in solitude. Time is our enemy when we are lonely. We are nostalgic about our past, anxious about our future, and find our present uncomfortable. The pleasure and freedom of solitude involve lack of concern about time. Because the present is sufficient, we either forget or embrace time as a friend. Work is not excluded. Sarton is going to try to write her poem, but she is not anxious. Some of our times are quite the opposite in that we are so anxious to achieve something that we fail over and over until it becomes clear that we should stop our labors. Later on, we revive the attempt, and it succeeds easily, because we are not so concerned about future success. We can be like the end in football who is so concerned about how he will run the ball after the pass that he fails to catch it in the first place. Solitude is attending to the present moment and letting the future take care of itself. As Sarton observes, it is a "time to be."

*What Solitude Is: Recognition of Relationship*

Solitude is recognition of relationship. Loneliness can be unending, but if we discover that we are concerned, not just about self or other but about a relationship, we are moved into solitude. The very discovery that we have lost a relationship is, at the same time, a discovery of relationships and of their existence in our lives. Solitude is the new condition in which relationship is recognized. The same occurs when we move to solitude from the condition of companionship. It is a move from the action of relating to awareness of the relationship. Here, the very discovery that we have kept a relationship is, at the same time, a discovery of relationships and their existence in our lives. So from either direction we move into recognition of relationship. That this occurs while we are alone appears paradoxical. We will try to make sense of solitude by exploring its task, the role of physical absence and presence in awareness of relationship, and the consciousness of self in solitude.

The task of solitude is illustrated by the experience and attitude of May Sarton. She did not consider her year alone to be a time of vacation, relaxation, or gentle slumber. Nor was it to be a period of pure and total involvement in her work as a writer. Nor was she about to explore herself for the pleasure of it. In an essay on being alone and not lonely, she says that after she has been with people a lot, she becomes "full to the brim with experience that needs to be sorted out." After being alone for a while, her self emerges, "bringing back all I have recently experienced to be explored and slowly understood."[26] She expands on this basic understanding of solitude in the opening statement of her journal. Recall how the passage quoted above evoked such comfortable delight in the promise of freedom, creativity, and timelessness. Remembering this, read the following statement to see what the delight allows to occur.

> Begin here. It is raining. I look out on the maple, where a few leaves have turned yellow, and listen to Punch, the parrot, talking to himself and to the rain ticking gently against the windows. I am here alone for the first time in weeks, to take up my "real" life again at last. That is what is strange—that friends, even passionate love, are not my real life unless there is time alone in which to explore and to discover what is happening or has happened. Without the

interruptions, nourishing and maddening, this life
would become arid. Yet I taste it fully only when I
am alone here and "the house and I resume old conversations."[27]

Solitude is a condition of exploring what has happened or is happening in relationships. Rather than getting away from it all (or, them
all), solitude is getting right into the heart of the matter. Such "old
conversations" are comfortable, but not entirely so. Sarton spends
her year in solitude because of her difficulties in a passionate relationship with another human being, and the end of the year brought an
end to the relationship. Despite the delight and the freedom and the
timelessness, the task is difficult and serious. Indeed, there are times
when recognition of relationship is the most vital task possible. Sarton is a writer and quite self-conscious about her use of herself and
her relationships for her work. We are not as likely to be so aware
of our being alone in this way. And surely we are not in the habit
of taking a year off to explore relationships. Even so, we have our
own experiences. For example, how often is our talking to ourselves
really only that? Each psyche is a crowd with which we can become
fully engaged. We talk to others in our head, trying to make sense
of what is going on between us, sorting our difficulties and enjoying
delights, sometimes being surprised by new insights about ourselves,
others, and the relationships. At times we try to enter this condition
deliberately, feeling the need for understanding. At other times we
only realize we are in the condition after it has been going on awhile.
And when solitude is occurring quite fully, there are surprises about
relationship that happen to us. We think about someone we have not
thought about in years. We miss someone more than we knew before. We discover we no longer feel as we did about someone. When
solitude rules, we are surprised by attitudes and insights that simply
pop into our consciousness. These are our recognitions of relationship. They may be painful or joyous, strong or weak, sure or uncertain. But whatever the case, there is a quality of discovery about them
to which we respond with "Aha." And the fundamental discovery is
that we are not alone in our aloneness.

We can understand this task of discovery and exploration of relationship better by looking at the occurrence of it with and without
the presence of the person to whom we are related. Consider the
attraction between people which occasionally occurs "across a

crowded room." Without some kind of presence, no relationship happens. But there is a difference between occurrence and discovery. The latter is a consequence of reflection, whereas the former can take place without consciousness. We can meet each other and establish a relationship unwittingly. Then afterward, sometimes long afterward, one of us suddenly discovers that the relationship exists. Or the occurrence and discovery can happen nearly simultaneously. Even in the latter case, discovery involves a separation from the event in which we momentarily stand back and realize what happened. This can take place in a brief moment of recognition. Whether or not our partner to the relationship is physically present is not so crucial. Occurrence and discovery of relationship are distinct. So also are physical presence and exploration of relationship. We often interact without contemplation of our activity. In solitude, we can recall events and explore the possibilities of fostering and guiding what happens. We can do this with or without the physical presence of the other.

The amount of time involved in a period of solitude varies considerably. Discovery and exploration are likely to be brief, disconnected moments when two people are physically together, and likely to be more extended when they are apart. Consequently, we have tended to ignore such moments when they occur in the presence of others. But they are just as real, valid, and useful then as they are when we are physically apart. Our image of solitude as a lengthy condition occurring under special circumstances of isolation obscures its frequent, however intermittent, presence in our lives. We move back and forth between occurrence and discovery, acting and exploring many times during a single, short meeting with the other. And the work of solitude when we are separate for a length of time may depend greatly on the solitude we have experienced while in the presence of the other. It seems likely that recognition of relationship is fostered most by physical presence and physical absence in alternation. With permanent presence, the distance of reflection is hampered. With permanent absence, there is little to reflect upon. So we should consider solitude as linked closely to the alternation of presence and absence.

This conclusion applies to other realms of relationship as well. We do not discover and explore our relationship with a tree only in its presence, but in both its presence and its absence. To see a flower only when it is present makes us bad poets and bad companions. So we discover and explore our relationship with society while in its midst and are actively involved as well as when we are contemplating it in the tranquillity of our study. And we can discover and explore our relationship with the world as a whole—with God, Humanity, Life, or whatever—in both its presence and its absence. Think about what has happened to you while reading this book. If you have been doing the exercises, and have been reading intermittently, then you have probably been alternating in and out of the presence of people and things you have been reflecting about. Indeed, one purpose of this book is to foster solitude.

To complete our initial understanding of solitude, we examine the role of the self. This is necessary because we have some tendency to see this condition as one of self-discovery. But the focus of solitude is not the self or the world, but the relationship between them. Further, even explorations of the self are about relationship. The psychologist who explores her dreams without awareness of how they relate to her social world will seriously limit her understanding of the unconscious. The historian who explores a past generation without awareness of how he is relating to that realm from his present self will seriously limit his understanding of the past. The self as self is opaque. The world as world is opaque. Only through relation can we understand either. Therefore it follows that solitude does not involve loss of either self or world.[28] Rather, we gain in our appreciation of the distinctiveness of the self, the world, and the relationship. This is quite different from loneliness. When we suffer our aloneness, separation may overwhelm all possible delight in uniqueness. The blind and terrified search for the lost person or thing fosters attempts to merge the other into the self or the self into the other, a panicky grasping and incorporating so that loss can never recur. One party is absorbed and dominated by the other in a dictatorship that is not even benevolent. The lonely are the authoritarian, whether they are dictators or slaves. Uniqueness is not deemed worth the price of separation. In the condition of solitude, however, separateness is used for the appreciation of distinctiveness. So the self is neither ignored nor elevated. This is because solitude is about relationship per se and about specific relationships, never about the self in isolation.

*Conclusion*

Now we go back to the approach we used at the beginning of our exploration of loneliness. Take pencil and paper and write at the top of the sheet: "My Own Solitude." Write a statement of no more than one hundred words on a personal experience of solitude. Tell the experience in narrative form. Do not worry about spelling, grammar, or literary merit. Select an experience you would not mind sharing with anyone else. Indeed, it would be helpful if you could do this exercise with several other persons so you could share and discuss the variety of responses. Take ten minutes right now to write your narrative.

Having taken this basic step in looking at your own solitude, you can ask yourself these questions about it.

1. To what extent and in what ways did the experience involve recognition of relationship?
2. To what extent and in what ways did it involve delight, freedom, creativity, and timelessness?
3. What was the length of time involved?
4. Did it occur in the presence or absence of the person(s) or thing(s) involved?
5. Did you enter this condition from loneliness or from companionship?
6. Did the experience have any negative effects?
7. What did it teach you about relationship per se?
8. What did it teach you about your own relationships?

It has probably taken you longer to write the narrative and answer the questions than to read this chapter. Solitude does require a leisurely attitude. And it requires hard work strangely combined with a relaxed openness to whatever might occur. If you have encountered solitude during this exercise, you have been alone and yet not alone because of your recognition of relationship. Swift is reported to have observed that "a wise man is never less alone than when he is alone."[29] From our perspective, the wiser we are, the less alone, because we are all the more aware of our relationships.

# CHAPTER VI

# *Discoveries Through Solitude*

Solitude is the way of being alone in which we recognize relationship. We make these discoveries in the five realms. The purpose of this chapter is to explore more fully our own creative use of solitude in discoveries of people, nature, and the holy.

## People

Some of our thought about a loved one in his or her absence is a matter of longing for reunion and thus is a symptom of loneliness. But this is not always so. We can reflect on a loved one with enjoyment of the occasion of physical separation precisely because it fosters awareness of the amazing love and the wonderful characteristics of our loved one. Absence makes our heart grow fonder, not in loneliness but in solitude. This occurs most enjoyably when we know reunion will occur shortly. It can also happen when reunion is not possible. After separation that is due to death, for example, loneliness occurs first, but as the loss is explored, loneliness is replaced by appreciation of the loved one and of the relationship per se. Eventually the meaning and value of the relationship become overwhelmingly real, actually as if the relationship has been discovered for the first time. In various occasions of permanent loss, there is a movement from preoccupation over the loss of the object to a new appreciation of the relationship. When this happens, grief is ended. The grief process can be understood as a movement from loneliness to solitude.

Our solitude can include discoveries about groups of people. When we talk to ourselves, we hold conversation with a whole host of others. This occurs when we are lonely, as we seek their presence to comfort and reassure us, but we call upon them in solitude also as companions to reflect along with us. Consider a theoretical scientist working alone on a formula to deal with newly observed phenomena that do not fit current theory. Some of the time he is so engaged in his project that he is quite unaware of self and others. But at other times he is quite conscious of his views and those of the theoretical community of his discipline. He is listening to them, debating with them, and constructing a response for them. At these moments, he may have little desire for personal contact, yet he is quite alert to their thinking, making discoveries about it, and perhaps is even surprised at how important they and their thoughts are to him. We do the same, calling in a group of our peers when we wonder what to do about our children or about a problem on the job. And, if we are alert, we learn something about these colleagues who appear in our heads.

Discoveries occur to us about the generations also. The significant persons in our past and future appear. We speak to them directly and imagine their response, or we speak to ourselves as they might speak to us. Because of such speaking, new understandings occur. Therefore, our historical world is fluid and actual changes in our relationship happen, even though the people involved may have been dead for years. This is not the case in loneliness, for there we are only trying to recover a relationship or a substitute for it. Loneliness is a conservative condition which attempts to stop change. In solitude we are reflecting on relationship, and change is encouraged, so new understanding of the family and the generations is endless.

This historical world is as large as our imaginations. We can discover the past of our society, even the past of the human race. We need not be scholars or philosophers, but stumble upon our first potshard while tramping the hills of the Southwest or explore an old building or find an antique piece of furniture in an urban environment. And we can discover our future. We have curiosity and interest, not out of anxiety of loneliness, but out of agreeable anticipation. Our lack of data about the future may be a factor that makes the past more an object of our solitude. But those of us who can really muse supply our own objects. To discover the future as a companion is a great and necessary gift. To have a sense that the future exists for us is an antidote to despair, and to discover that the future exists even more for others is the gateway to community. Our intimation of this future is developed more fully and concretely in solitude. The imagination creates scenarios that take on a life of their own. Our future as companion may be good, bad, or neutral, but it has a shape and character that can be engaged in planning, revision, congratulations, chagrin, and the like.

This engagement with the generations creates people who are intermediaries between us and the whole of human history—our saints. We have our religious saints, such as Joan of Arc, and our social saints, such as Martin Luther King. And we have saints within certain areas of life. George Bernard Shaw has a dying artist affirm his creed:

> I believe in Michaelangelo, Velásquez, and Rembrandt; the might of design, the mystery of color, the redemption of all things by Beauty everlasting, and the message of Art that has made these hands blessed. Amen. Amen.[30]

Lawyers and doctors and others have their own selections of professional saints. We also have our personal saints, however secret or hardly recognized by us they are. They are people in the present or the past who are of special significance to us because they embody experience and contributions that enable us both to see ourselves as we want to be seen and to act as we want to act. They are guides who affirm and lead us. They are shepherds who heal us when we are sick at heart, sustain us when we need consolation, guide us when we need direction, and reconcile us when we are out of sorts with our lives. These heroes may be figures from our personal, national, or cultural past, or they may never have lived other than in imagination. In solitude our saints come to life as models for identity and saviors of life. They are companions who know the way, and we can go, perhaps only go, where they have been. Consider all that has been said in Christian Scripture about Jesus Christ as the companion of all human beings. What is said about him is what is reflected in our more informal and equally powerful attachment to personal saints. To be alone with our saints in solitude is to discover relationships with the generations that foster living.

Consider now how you have encountered people in solitude. Take time to remember the following occasions. Note each with a few concrete words and comment on what you learned about yourself, your companion, and your relationship.

1. Recall a time alone when you explored your relationship with a loved one enjoyably. What did you discover?
2. Recall a time alone when you explored a relationship in which separation was permanent. What did you discover?
3. Recall a time alone when you held a discussion with a group of peers or colleagues. What did you discover?
4. Recall a time alone when you found a part of the distant past to be your companion. What did you discover?
5. Recall a time alone when you found a part of the future to be your companion. What did you discover?
6. List your personal saints.
7. Under what circumstances do these saints come to mind and how do they help you?

*Nature*

In solitude we can be surprised by things. On the way home from a long walk in the cold, a warm recall of our house is a most pleasurable and reassuring recognition of a companion that is waiting for our return. We may see a particular painting many times, study it, just spend time in its presence, talk about it with others, and even read about it in order to know about its meaning to the artist and its place in art history. When this process goes on, the painting can, at some specific moment, be discovered as a companion. Automobiles, sculptures, books may suddenly leap into our minds and hearts for recognition, and we know that a new awareness is achieved with them just as it can be with people.

A traditional realm of discovery in solitude has been nature. We are easily reminded by Henry David Thoreau that nature can be our companion. His essay on solitude in *Walden* opens with recollection of those times in which we walk out into a pleasant evening by ourselves and forget all our human concerns with people and are totally attentive to whatever Nature is doing with its light, air, plants, and animals.[31] We are not alone, but find ourselves in company. And when nature appears to respond, the recognition is highlighted. Thoreau notes:

> I once had a sparrow alight upon my shoulder for a
> moment while I was hoeing in a village garden, and
> I felt that I was more distinguished by that circum-

stance than I should have been by any epaulet I
could have worn.[32]

When nature takes a step toward us we are surprised, impressed, and
flattered. The "dumber" the animal, the more impressed we are.
More difficult to appreciate, but very powerful, is the glimpse of a
flower bowing toward us in the breeze. With the plant seeming to
engage us, we are removed from the domesticated and see the relationship involving nature herself.

The natural things discovered in solitude are usually quite friendly
to us. Yet all recognition of relation is somewhat perilous. In the
object realm the companion discovered can be frightening. This may
occur in places that are alien—a vast expanse of desert or sea, a pond
or pit that appears bottomless, or an unusually shaped peak that
appears to have been deliberately fashioned by more than natural
erosion. We do not pass by such places alertly without some kind of
acknowledgment that organizes the strangeness. Like earlier peoples,
we may tell a story about it, so that the place becomes a companion.
Even fear of an evil companion is preferred to the terror of the totally
strange.

In between nature as domestic or strange lies the challenging companion we recognize when we climb mountains or sail the seas in
small craft. The relationship is that of competition with mutual respect. A person who reaches the top of Mt. Everest does win in the
contest with fellow human beings by being the first of the group
(although it is not polite to mention it). But the battle with the
mountain is not won. We do not conquer Everest, because mutual
respect fosters humility and concern for the companion itself. After
all, one must climb down from the top and may want to climb again.
The battle is never won with any challenging companion—human or
otherwise. We who take far less challenging relationships with nature notice this also. The place we reach or the path we travel
becomes recognized by us as a companion we recall and/or return to
for sustenance. In such relationships the two parties are equal and the
challenge is from both.

We become separated from nature, from one of its objects, and
then there is search because of loneliness. City dwellers who miss the
nature experienced in earlier years or in vacation times seek to recover relationship through animals and plants in the apartment and
observation of wildlife in the park. But loneliness can occur in the

midst of nature as well. The physical presence of nature does not assure relationship with it. Farmers vary in their response to nature just as urban office workers vary in their response to people. Solitude in this realm, like any other, is an achievement. It is a profound experience which does not necessarily occur when we are sunbathing, backpacking, or bird-watching. Or it may occur and pass nearly unnoticed. You have probably had moments of discovery with nature that were hardly recognized and not explored at all. When we are surprised by the things of nature, we know it by the awful joy that occurs.

It is appropriate now to recall our own discoveries of relationship in the realm of nature. This is not an exercise just for avowed lovers of nature. They may not relate to nature in solitude very often, and those not particularly interested in nature consciously may well have such experiences. Be sure to comment on what you have learned about yourself, nature, and your relationship.

1. Recall a time alone when some aspect of nature became significant to you. What did you discover?
2. Recall a time alone when some aspect of nature became significant in a frightening way. What did you discover?
3. Recall a time alone when some aspect of nature became significant as a challenging companion. What did you discover?
4. Recall a time alone when it was likely that you failed to recognize a moment of possible discovery with nature. What got in the way?
5. In what ways, if any, do you seek out nature as a companion?

### The Holy

Our contemporaries are likely to connect solitude with discovery of self, but tradition is clearly inclined to recognize it as connected with discovery of God. By either wandering from one place to another or residing in an out-of-the-way place, a person seeks and establishes aloneness. The goal is not privacy but company, the discovery of relationship with the world as a whole, whether it is labeled "Spirit," "Suchness," "Being," or the "Holy." The American Plains Indian seeks and endures aloneness until he is granted a vision that will be his companion for the rest of his life, a vision without which he cannot live as a true adult. The classical Christian believer leaves learning and community for the desert to discover and be maintained by the God discovered in isolation and silence. Solitude and the sacred are closely allied. Indeed, solitude is such a remarkable experience and so different from either loneliness or companionship, as well as from such other states of aloneness as stupor, narcissism, or busyness, that it partakes of the holy whenever fully experienced.

This link between solitude and the holy has been noted most usefully by Alfred North Whitehead. He writes:

> Religion is what the individual does with his own solitariness. It runs through three stages, if it evolves to its final satisfaction. It is the transition from God the void to God the enemy, and from God the enemy to God the companion. Thus religion is solitariness; and if you are never solitary, you are never religious. . . .
> In its solitariness the spirit asks, What, in the way of value, is the attainment of life? And it can find no such value till it has merged its individual claim with that of the objective universe. Religion is world-loyalty.[33]

The first sentence in the quotation is duly famous as a definition, and the concept of stages is a useful one to apply to any of our discoveries and explorations in solitude. We do not find "instant" companions in any realm of relationship, but strangers who can become friends. It is the last sentence that is most in accord with the definition proposed in this book, religion being defined as attending to relationship with the world. "World-loyalty" is manifest in religion. What tends to elevate solitude in our thinking is the mood that accompanies discovery of relationship. It is the revelation to human beings. All revelation is, whatever its guise, essentially identical in message. Revelation is always revelation of relationship. The revelation is that relationship is. Life at any level depends upon it for survival, and human life is not different, except in that its capacity for consciousness makes awareness of this necessity possible. Samuel Johnson made a celebrated remark to the woman who ventured to accept the universe: "Gad, she had better!" This is clever and limited. This is the task, but it is not automatic for us and not automatically maintained. So loss of world acceptance occurs and so does rediscovery of it in solitude. It is this necessity, and the awareness of it, which renders the mood of solitudinal discovery so powerfully positive. "World-loyalty" means that relationship rules and, therefore, that we can relate to individuals, groups, the generations, objects, and to the world itself. To encounter the holy is to discover relationship as necessary and possible.

The oneness of the revelation of relationship is seen by us in different ways. Some of us do so traditionally with reference to God. Thomas Merton speaks first of solitude and silence, of entrusting oneself to this silence that is beyond all relationships.[34] But the silence that seems first to be only an absence is finally a presence. For Merton, solitude is communion. He says:

> Solitude has to be objective and concrete. It has to be a communion in something greater than the world, as great as Being itself, in order that in its deep peace we may find God.[35]

He says this even more paradoxically: "As soon as you are really alone, you are with God."[36] To leave behind all relationships in solitude is to have the possibility of recognition of relationship with the world as a whole. It is the discovery of the world as companion, and we traditionally call it "God." Those of us who are firmly within a religious tradition can have this experience of the holy and be quite comfortable with the usual way of speaking of it.

Our discovery of relationship in solitude can also occur without reference to God or to any other traditional words and concepts. The focus can be on people, on our personal and social saints, or on humanity itself. The autobiographical reflections of a wise old woman, Florida Scott-Maxwell, contain such humanistic theology. Read this passage carefully to discover if you have had similar revelations.

> It feels right to take humanity into my heart, or out of my heart and examine it and be eased of it. Poor, poor mankind what a marvel it is, what marvels man has done. His buildings alone would make one assume him an archangel. His music, his order, the richness of his acts—it is because of marvels accomplished that we have hope—and when man refused much of the time to live up to the range of the mighty creature he sometimes is, then hopeful people like me make a to-do. When we see what mankind can do, and be—and we have no idea why it is

so much easier to do than to be—and when with
equal clarity we see what he usually is, then child-
ishly, shamefully we cry, "Won't more people be
strong, and wise and lovable, because I try and
can't." Yet even in my despair I see man rise to such
noble heights in his fateful struggle that more often
than we guess the gods may regard him with broth-
erly awe.[37]

She sees and responds to humankind as a whole. It is her companion
with whom she struggles. Some of us are religious humanists like this
wherein humankind is our ultimate concern and companion. We
have moments of humble awe about this strange beast's existence in
the universe that renew our capacity to relate.

Discovery of the world as a whole also occurs through nature.
Thoreau's discussion often indicates a nature mysticism. When asked
if he is not lonely, he responds that he lives where we all want to
dwell, near to "the perennial source of our life."[38] Walden Pond
points beyond itself to the whole of existence for Thoreau. A quite
different context for such discovery is given in Admiral Byrd's record
of his six months alone in Antarctica.[39] Following the progression
Whitehead mentions, nature becomes a powerful companion, at first
malevolent, but then benevolent. He does refer to a blizzard as a
vindictive enemy which disintegrates one's world.[40] But in and
through such experiences of chaos and evil, he comes to a realization
of the existence of the world and his relationship to it. Speaking of
the processes of the cosmos, he writes:

> In that instant I could feel no doubt of man's oneness
> with the universe. The conviction came that rhythm
> was too orderly, too harmonious, too perfect to be a
> product of blind chance—that, therefore, there must
> be purpose in the whole and that man was part of
> that whole and not an accidental offshoot. It was a
> feeling that transcended reason; that went to the
> heart of man's despair and found it groundless. The
> universe was a cosmos, not a chaos; man was right-
> fully a part of that cosmos as were the day and
> night.[41]

What is important here is not the intellectual conviction Byrd affirms,
but his experience of this "rhythm" of the harmony of the whole and
his relationship to it. When chaos becomes cosmos, the world as a

whole is being discovered through nature. Like Thoreau or Byrd, we too can survey the heavens or fields of grass with an inner vision provided by solitude which somehow communicates to us that everything is "all right." We experience that ultimate well-being we dimly realize is the source and support of our well-being in relationship to the various parts of the world.

Our discoveries of the holy will vary considerably in the parts of the world by which they are revealed and in the language we choose to respond with. Some of us will make much of such experiences, while others will make little, but most of us do experience the world as a whole and so have some sense of what we mean by "holy." So, not as a matter of piety, but as one more of our exercises to understand the nature of ourselves as human animals concerned about relationship, we consider the following questions.

1. Recall an experience, if you have had any, of the holy that would be considered by you as traditional, relating to God.
2. Recall an experience, if you have had any, of the holy that would be considered by you as humanistic, relating to humanity.
3. Recall an experience, if you have had any, of the holy that would be considered by you as relating to nature.
4. What is your preferred way of speaking about such experiences? Check one of the following: God. Humanistic. Nature. Other.
5. How important are such experiences of the holy to you in your life? Very important. Somewhat important. Not important.
6. Note down an issue about this understanding of the ultimate revelation as being revelation of relationship that you would like to discuss.

### Conclusion

Solitude is the discovery that we are not alone. I hope you have used this chapter and its exercises to explore those occasions in which you discovered people, nature, and the holy. If you did, the paradox of solitude will not have been dispelled, but rendered more real and mysterious. Our next step is mundane, but just as crucial—exploration of the problems we have with solitude.

# CHAPTER VII

# *Difficulties with Our Own Solitude*

The mood of loneliness is so overwhelmingly negative that its dynamics must be explored for us to see its positive nature. The mood of solitude tends to be in the other direction. Recognition of relationship is of such value that we can accept solitude uncritically as both pleasant and beneficial. But that recognition may bring into consciousness material about ourselves and others which is painful. Further, it can be so disruptive to both ourselves and others that it is destructive of relationship. So in this chapter we explore the difficulties we have with our own solitude.

## Entering Solitude

The first difficulty we have is entering solitude. Society can see it as only a negative flight from reality and responsibility. We can behave this way, wishing to escape the pain of loneliness by a quick leap into companionship without ever experiencing the pain of recognition and contemplation of relationship. "If in relationship to others, stay that way. If out of relationship, get back into it fast." This is how we speak to ourselves. So both we and our friends can work together to defeat solitude.

The battles we have in entering solitude are depicted well in the fictional narrative *The Left-Handed Woman* by Peter Handke.[42] Marianne leaves her husband and loneliness ensues. She does not want to leap into relationships, but other people encourage this: her husband tells her not to be too much alone; a woman friend shares her own despair at being alone; her publisher tries to use her loneliness for his own sexual and loneliness gratification; her husband threatens her with the fears of growing old and unattractive; a young man declares his love and wants reciprocation; and, perhaps worst of all, her father visits, exposing his own loneliness and asserting that she will end up in the same condition. But the real threat is from Marianne herself. She masters it by the end of the story when the people gather, uninvited, for a party in her home. She realizes that she can listen to them and understand their loneliness and fear of it, and also their desire to lose themselves by means of her. The aftermath of this party is her first period of solitude. First, she is content to be alone. Then she becomes aware of herself and wiggles her toes. And then she gets pencil and paper and draws the situation she is in—her feet, the room in which she resides, the way out of it through the windows, and finally the night sky outside—the world.

The story of this "left-handed" woman, so sinister to her companions, is a reminder of the forces working against solitude and of the battle we must and do wage. When we fall out of relationship, we do not usually fall into solitude, but into loneliness. Then there is much in society and ourselves that encourages our flight from loneliness. Think of all the well-meaning people who have encouraged us to flee. Marianne could have fled into a self-satisfied individualism and quite simply ignored or mistreated her friends. Or she could have fled into the thoughtless two-person relationship of an affair. This is what we are tempted to do when we hurt through loss of self-esteem. But she did neither and remained vulnerable. The result was recognition of relationship. She became alert to herself and to others, especially to how those others related. She is wiser about the relationships than they are. When we resist the temptation to flee, solitude occurs and our self-esteem becomes based on the reality of our wisdom about relationship and the battle we have fought.

The conclusion is that solitude is not handed to us on a platter. Or if it is, the gift is easily declined. Solitude is entered with difficulty. Make your own record of this by considering the following experiences you have had.

1. Recall an occasion when you were lonely and leaped into a relationship ill-advisedly. What did you gain and what did you lose?
2. Recall an occasion when you resisted the temptation to flee

loneliness and did enter solitude. What did you gain and what did you lose?

3. Recall the attitudes of your friends and/or loved ones on both of the above occasions. How did they help and hurt your feelings, thoughts, and behavior?

4. Recall your own feelings and thoughts on both of the above occasions. How did they influence your behavior?

### Staying in Solitude

The second problem we have with our own solitude is that of staying in it. To possess solitude and then lose it, and to possess it again and lose it—this is oscillation. It may not occur equally among us. Some of us may be like Thoreau, who claimed that he was lonely only once during his two years of solitude. Others of us may be more like Thomas Wolfe, who found solitude the rare condition.[43] But most of us probably experience a moving in and out of solitude which can be more upsetting than residing in one state or the other.

A single entry in the journal of May Sarton reflects our common experience.[44] It states that she was calmed by waking up to the sight of nature—a moment of solitude. She also refers to the isolation and loneliness of having left her lover at the end of the weekend. And then this entry, which opened with a beautiful statement about the nature she discovered on awakening, concludes with a different version. She acknowledges that she awakened in tears, wondering if it is possible to relate better to another human being. In this one entry about just a few moments of wakening, we find references to all three states: loneliness, solitude, and companionship. It is a courageous entry which reminds her and us of a movement that can be frighteningly rapid. The fact that she is in the midst of a floundering relationship is also a reminder to us of the variability of our conditions when this occurs. Uncertainty unfreezes our somewhat habitual stances in one of the three conditions and we are dismayed by the unaccustomed movement. This makes our solitude difficult to appreciate and use.

The moving in and out of solitude and loneliness occurs without such unrest in relationship. Florida Scott-Maxwell was eighty-two years of age when she wrote her reflections, *The Measure of My Days.* [45] She is an impressive human being, seeming to possess a high degree of independence, concern for others, discipline, flexibility, reflective-

ness, and creativity. Indeed, her reflections give rise to the image of
the wise old woman. Such a person does not need the continual
presence of other people to stimulate her and prevent boredom. She
can entertain herself. Further, she can respect herself, that is, see
herself as possessing depths and mysteries to be explored. No doubt
such a reflective individual actually requires much time and space
alone to be at all content. Solitude for her should be an opportunity
and a blessing. But Scott-Maxwell does not find her situation
straightforward. As a true reflective person, she can write:

> What fun it is to generalize in the privacy of a note-
> book. It is as I imagine waltzing on ice might be. A
> great delicious sweep in one direction, taking your
> full strength, and then with no trouble at all, an
> equally delicious sweep in the opposite direction.[46]

This is sweet solitude. Moreover, her notebook is filled with fine
insight into age and human relationships. The solitude is creative.
But after she has written about "waltzing on ice," the very next
sentence is: "My notebook does not help me think, but it eases my
crabbed heart."[47] Throughout, the notebook gives ample evidence of
the mood of the old to have done with the busyness and frenzy of
adult society. She gives full data on herself as a person who has great
capacities for solitude, and it does occur for her. Yet it is not a
continuous state, but is contaminated by loneliness, and by the allied
conditions of isolation, alienation, depression, and grief. Solitude is
a difficult achievement, even for those who are most capable of it and
are not in the midst of relationships that are changing drastically.
Scott-Maxwell reminds us that our battle with loneliness is never
fully won, but is fought over and over again against strong odds by
means of our endurance and courage.

   The conclusion is that, after tasting solitude and the recognition of
relationship, we lose solitude to loneliness and then can regain it
again. We oscillate. No doubt we would prefer to rest in either
condition. Indeed, we might suspect ourselves when we claim that
this is actually what we do. It is possible that we do oscillate but that
we refuse to recognize this uncomfortable movement. We are never
finished with loneliness, and solitude remains sweet because recognition of relationship is the prize. So the movement in and out of
solitude remains typical for us. What can sour solitude most is the
expectation that such oscillation can be avoided.

It is appropriate now to record your own experience with this movement in and out of solitude.

1. Recall an occasion when you were oscillating between solitude and loneliness.
2. With just a few words, note down your feelings, thoughts, and behavior on this occasion.
3. Recall an occasion, either the above or another, when you tried to avoid or get out of such an oscillation.
4. What did you gain and lose by this attempt?
5. When you are moved into oscillation, which habitual condition is being broken up? Loneliness. Solitude. Both.

### Leaving Solitude

It is not surprising that we cling to solitude in order to avoid loneliness. But it may surprise us that some prefer solitude to companionship. We do have different degrees of need to be physically and psychically present with other people and things in companionship. But the relational action of companionship, the actual doing with another person or thing, is a necessity for all of us. So solitude is not a final goal in which one can rest permanently. It is the discovery of a new perspective in which concern for either self or other is replaced by concern for the relationship per se between two parties. This discovery moves us out into actual connections, prompting its own end by returning us to old relationships and turning us to new ones. For solitude to be perpetual with regard to any specific relationship would be avoidance of either the loneliness of separation or the companionship of relational action. Nevertheless, we are not above trying for such permanency now and then.

We are familiar with the observation that some of us love people in general but not in particular. Something similar occurs when we prefer to discover and contemplate relationships rather than be actively engaged in them. We remain specifically focused but permanently disengaged. This occurs in the romantic lover who enjoys the loved one all the more when he or she is absent. Absence makes the heart grow fonder, and the return of the person can be a letdown. In romantic love, the condition can be enjoyed more than the person, and even the person can be loved more at a distance than close up. The discovery and exploration of the relationship that occurs in

solitude is made permanent, as long as the loved one tolerates it. If
two persons are in love the same way, the romance can last longer.
It is as if both are mistaking the other's eyeball for their own navel.
As children can play side by side without really being connected, so
two adults can be exploring a love relationship in solitude without
being present to each other. This is not all bad and it can be useful,
but it is likely to be misleading. It is parallel solitude. It seems likely
that much early relationship between two adolescents, for example,
could involve a high percentage of such solitude with a small and safe
amount of companionship. If one partner changes and seeks the
actual action of companionship, trouble occurs. In the relationships
of older adults, this trouble can be severe. The one who dwells on the
relationship without acting on it will come to be perceived as distant
if not deceptive. And the deceptive one may wonder why the loved
one is so misunderstanding. "I am thinking about you all the time.
How could you be offended?" The distance is seen by the one but
not by the other. Such solitude in a long-term relationship is not
creative.

It may be that some of us are prone to this attempt to remain in
solitude and avoid the concreteness of relationship. We must think
flexibly about this and mention more than just those who devote
their life to prayer before God or to laboratory experimentation for
the sake of science. Those of us who write about people may also
belong in this category. May Sarton says that she has been accused
of being disloyal when she talks about human situations in which she
and others she knows are involved.[48] She disagrees, arguing that she
is not using the experiences for her own ends, but for her shared
meditation with her readers, who can learn from the recorded experiences. She does not want to be discreet because, as she says, "My
business is the analysis of feelings."[49] This is just what goes on in
solitude. She is loyal to it more than to companionship itself. This
seems a likely condition for writers who explore relationships. That
we gain by their focus does not mean that they do not lose.

We can also speculate about those of us who work professionally
with and for people. Consider, for example, the psychotherapist. He
or she is exposed to actual relationships with other human beings.
But this is a one-way affair wherein the patient relates to the therapist as a human being in a more normal fashion than the therapist
can to the patient. Further, the therapist focuses on recognition of
their relationship, what it is and how it works, matters of transfer-

ence, countertransference, and the like. The task of therapists, I suggest, is to get into and remain in the condition of solitude. Solitude is their tool for understanding and helping. They enter into the work with this understanding of the method. The patient has to learn the method. So we can understand solitude as a way of defining the peculiar nature of psychotherapy. It is a form of parallel solitude in which one teaches the other to reach it and use it. Therapists serve us well by this method. Whether they serve themselves as well is another question, especially if the need for solitude is so strong as to nearly eliminate the need for companionship. Of course, we need not be professional helpers of people to be prone to solitude in this way. Those of us who are informally helpful to others in our lives may be equally or even more dedicated to remaining within solitude.

Finally, we should beware of having a romance with solitude. Old foolish talk about being together is matched by some more recent foolish talk about being alone. As this chapter is being written, our society is making much of living alone and enjoying it, whether one is young or old, widowed or single. Surely we can be single and satisfied, and living with another human being, in or out of marriage, is less than continual delight. But we should be concerned lest solitude and/or loneliness are actually enemies rather than friends, and the victim is making the best of a bad situation by identifying with the aggressor—an "If you can't lick 'em, join 'em" attitude. The mood can be like that of Thomas Wolfe. This young author asserted that he could respect but not follow the life of love. He speaks of loneliness, probably meaning solitude, in this song of praise:

> Loneliness forever and the earth again! Dark brother and stern friend, immortal face of darkness and of night, with whom the half part of my life was spent, and with whom I shall abide now till my death forever—what is there for me to fear as long as you are with me? . . . Come to me, brother.[50]

May we not ask, at least, if Wolfe has a romance going with solitude that is unnecessarily limited? When we speak this way, we are probably protecting ourselves against the threats of companionship or the lack of it. This is a useful ploy if we do not persist in it.

Solitude is useful. It is even a good for those who prefer to dwell in it to the near exclusion of the other two conditions. But our conclusion is that those who are so tempted should consider the danger of having such distance from companionship become an aloneness that is not solitude and is less than human. How could recognition of relationship with an individual, in discovery and exploration, continue without the stimulation of companionship with the individual? Explore your own experience by making the observations directed below.

1. Recall an occasion when you tried to avoid leaving solitude.
2. In just a few words, note down your feelings, thoughts, and behavior on this occasion.
3. What did you gain and lose by this attempt?
4. Recall an occasion when you left solitude freely for companionship.
5. In just a few words, note down your feelings, thoughts, and behavior on this occasion.
6. What did you gain and what did you lose by this movement from solitude to companionship?

### Conclusion

These three difficulties involved in solitude concern the major issue of dealing with loneliness and companionship while in solitude. There is no simple movement into solitude, no simple remaining in solitude, and no simple leaving of solitude. Solitude, being recognition of relationship, is sweet. But since life is complicated, it is a bittersweetness. Perhaps this is why we may prefer other ways of being alone without being lonely. Solitude is rewarding because it is demanding. Some of these demands are reflected in the following:

1. Which one of the three difficulties is most revealed by your behavior? Entering. Remaining. Leaving.
2. What do you enjoy most in your solitude?
3. What do you enjoy least in your solitude?
4. What difficulties do you experience in solitude other than those discussed in this chapter?
5. Recall the three different ways of being alone without being lonely which we discussed in the last chapter. Make an estimate of the percentage of your total time alone without being lonely that you are in solitude. Estimate the percentage of total time you are alone in each of the other three ways of being alone but not lonely.

# CHAPTER VIII

# *Difficulties with the Solitude of Others*

Solitude is the recognition of relationship and is as valuable for the human spirit as breathing is for the body. It is a powerful experience and can be destructive. We may seek solitude, or seek to remain in it, by doing our best to exclude both loneliness and companionship from our lives. Even with respect for these other conditions, we face the danger of discovering and exploring relationship in such a way that specific relationships are destroyed. This damage can be caused by a lover who is more in love with love itself and with his image of the loved one that with the loved one herself as a companionable reality. Or it can be caused by a mother who is more interested in parenting than in her specific child, or more interested in research on her child than in mutual enjoyment with her child. In these and similar situations, solitude rules over companionship, and specific relationships are endangered. Yet the insight and relational enthusiasm of solitude is valuable. How can one explore relationship without destroying it?

### Solitude as Disruptive

Despite our own enjoyment of solitude, we can easily see that others may be upset by solitude, and it is also easy for us to recall our own difficulties with the solitude of others. What appears to be solitude may actually be other ways of being alone without being lonely, either a reclusiveness or a narcissism, to such an extent that it justifies labels of irresponsibility or sickness. Or the solitude may be genuine but chronic, failing to move us toward actual relational action in companionship. Further, genuine and limited solitude may well provoke anxiety in those who observe it and who have ambivalent and concealed need to do the same. So there are many legitimate and serious reasons to be concerned about the solitude of someone else that occurs in our midst. But the crucial problem lies in the fact that solitude, however genuine and limited, remains a disruption. We should never consider it otherwise. When it occurs in the very young and the very old, it does not threaten society, but its occurrence in the fully involved adult is a natural threat. Those of us who savor solitude should understand its effect on others and on our own relationships as fully as possible.

Consider some of the possibilities of disruption in the realm of relationship with an individual—lover, friend, parent, or child. If a husband, for example, discovers depth—his need for relationship per se—but does not discover breadth, there is the likelihood of a new clinging to the relationship that overburdens, if not bores, the partner. Or if he discovers breadth in intimate relations without discovery of depth, the partner may be deserted or become a member of a contemporary harem. Likewise, a spouse may discover and explore a different realm of relationship, such as that of nature or of the world as a whole, and be so involved in the discovery and exploration of it that the realm of relationship to individuals is left far behind, and so the partner is abandoned in spirit. Finally, there are those who have avoided solitude all their adult lives and then move into it with a totalism that removes them from intimacy altogether. Such people may simply "take off" for a different place and for a length of time that leaves the partner without companionship. These are all examples of a solitude that is valid but limited. The limitations disrupt. But even perfect solitude is disruptive. Discovery and exploration of relationship per se are troublesome because they are likely to upset the status quo. Of course, solitude can be especially disruptive of any companionship in which the focus is on physical presence, continuing demonstration of affection, and maintenance of the relationship just as it is without change. Solitude does not support these elements directly, for it requires distancing, this being neither openly demonstrative of one's concern for another nor openly encouraging of the relationship. Solitude does support the growth and development of relationship, but this, of course, is disruptive to a relationship that wards off change. So it is the perversions of solitude, the limitations of solitude, and solitude itself that can endanger relationship. Like other valuable medicine, solitude can be a poison.

Because solitude is both valuable and dangerous, we learn how to experience it in ways that are not so threatening to others and to ourselves. Both the need and the fulfillment of it are disguised from others and sometimes from ourselves as well. We may go off fishing in order to catch fish, doze in the sun, or enjoy companionship with others; or we may go fishing in order to be in solitude. We may go off on a long walk for exercise and to find wildflowers, but also in quest of solitude. And we may return with flowers to show and an experience of solitude to conceal. The flowers indicate both that we have been "doing" something and that we are mindful of others. While some of us may know what we are doing in these covert approaches, others may not. Most likely, few of us know that we not only are seeking and enjoying solitude but also are developing and following routine ways of doing so that disguise our intentions. These routines are very important to us and to those closely related to us who would be disturbed if the disguises were absent and the solitude revealed. We are uncomfortable with a member of our family not wanting to be available to us, but are quite pleased to comment on a relative with a passion for playing the card game of solitaire. The number of activities we use that conceal our search for and the presence of solitude are innumerable: listening to music, apparent reading or television-watching, sunbathing, walking, jogging, napping, knitting, working in the garden, and other household chores, arriving at one's work early and/or staying late, and so on. There is much of our physical and mental activity that may be neither useful nor enjoyable in its own right but that actually serves in an extra fashion as the cover for our search for and delight in solitude.

Our need for solitude may be strong, and we may be lacking in imagination and disguises. Consider the middle-aged person who is fully involved with so many relationships—with both friends and colleagues who are of the peer generation, and with both children and parents who are of other generations. It has been noted that reflection is a striking characteristic of the middle-aged, and there is a strong need for conscious processing of all the data of relationship that are at hand and that sometimes overwhelm the individual.[51] Those who are the most involved with others are those who need a solid amount of time and space away from companionships for solitude. How can the middle-aged do so without destroying the relationships themselves? Solitude for more than a moment is not an easy achievement for those of us who are so enmeshed. We have not the time, nor does society approve if we try to take the time. So we give ourselves disguises. If this is not possible or is insufficient, the need for reflective attention to relationship becomes a pressure that may wreak havoc, as when a man quits his job to sail a craft across the sea, or a woman leaves her family in order to paint. Because this need for solitude is not supported by our society, it erupts and damages unnecessarily. Yet society withholds support because solitude does threaten relationships. This is the quandary of both the society which fears disruptiveness and the middle-aged who need solitude in order that the relationships can be developed creatively.

Consider now your own experience with solitude as disruptive.

1. Recall an occasion when the intent and/or practice of being alone (whether or not in actual solitude) by another person was disruptive for you. Note this occasion briefly and concretely.
2. What were your feelings, thoughts, and behavior in response to the situation?
3. How did your response affect the other person?
4. Did the person disguise the intent to be alone? If so, by what means?
5. Recall an occasion when your own intent and/or practice of being alone (whether or not in actual solitude) was disruptive for someone else. Note this occasion briefly and concretely.
6. What were, to the best of your knowledge, the feelings, thoughts, and behavior of the other person in response to the situation?
7. How did the other person's response affect you?
8. Did you disguise the intent to be alone? If so, by what means?
9. Recall an occasion when the actual solitude of another occurred and was disruptive for you. Note briefly your response to the situation, the effect of your response on the other person, and the disguise present.
10. Recall an occasion when your own actual solitude was disruptive for someone else. Note briefly the response to the situation, the effect of the response on you, and the disguise present.
11. What are your own typical disguises for being alone?

*Support for Solitude*

With regard to loneliness, companionship, and solitude, it is the last we should treat least casually. We do so especially by marking it off in time and space. We take care by formalizing and officially retreating. Recall Thoreau in his two years of solitude. He seems to make too much fuss about this formal retreat which is really not so much in solitude anyway. Or so it seems. But ritual is what all the fuss is about. He is marking out a most special condition that is to exist for a certain amount of time in a certain space. This sets limits for entering and leaving. It also makes the most of solitude as something special. These characteristics alert his neighbors and community that something different is going on. Society is informed and put on guard. So solitude is dangerous, but there is the possibility of understanding it as ritual action which may protect and support the individual and the society.

Ritual occurs to contain dangerous power. So, for example, meeting strangers is dangerous, and we respond to this by the custom of shaking hands. This gives us something to do that we can feel comfortable about and also shows that we are not concealing weapons. More extensive customs involve setting ourselves apart in time and space to function in a special way when we recognize danger. Kings and pregnant women are surrounded by extended customs that are due to this double concern of seeking both contact with the power and safety from it. Ritual invites us into the power, enables us to use it, and then to take it away with us—to actually get away with it and survive. Recall your own needs for formal occasions. Sometimes we are formal because that is the custom of our culture. Other times we find ourselves becoming, so to speak, informally formal. The formality is of our own, individual choosing. The chances are that we do this when we are aware of power and our dual need for its strength and for our safety.

Our ritual support for solitude may not have been as highly developed as protocol before royalty or as extended as that of Thoreau, but we are probably aware of having "taken off" from daily reality in a kind of reflective action. This is not a searching for relationship, but reflecting upon it. Most of us do not reflect only like philosophers with clear abstractions. Rather than mull over by removing ourselves totally from the situation, we think by means of acting and this action is done for the sake of the thinking involved. This is not the "acting out," which is thoughtless behavior, but the acting in solitude, which is thoughtful. For example, have you ever begun a relationship with someone for the purpose, not of developing the relationship itself, but of playing out some inner concern about relationship—sexuality, intimacy, expression of feelings, and so forth? Or, more simply, have you ever called up a friend to talk with, not to relate to as a companion, but to try out some relational possibility? We learn by doing, and do in order to learn. This is "taking off" in a most constructive sense.

If you can recall such reflective action, you can appreciate how it may have troubled your friend and hurt your relationship unless there was some special understanding of it. Misunderstanding often rules in these events. A spouse's reflective action of taking on a young lover can foster an unnecessary end to an established relationship rather than a renewal of it. The problem is twofold. First, the experience of relationship in solitude is taken as having literal, everyday meaning rather than symbolic meaning. What is really behavior in solitude is interpreted, quite naturally and nearly inevitably, as behavior in companionship. Secondly, the actual behavior is overly dramatic and forceful. This occurs partially because there is no formal, socially approved ritual support for solitude available, and the informal ritual is created out of high pressure and search for visibility. Following this example, a better ritual could relate an older woman with a young man and have the identical symbolic and solitudinal significance and power as does a brief affair that includes intimacy and sexual intercourse. Social relationships between such couples can be formalized by society in ways both controlling and encouraging. It happens, for example, in our work and community associations. When the symbolic activity of ritual rules, other relationships are not uselessly challenged.

The danger of solitude cannot be eliminated. The disruption that solitude causes is a consequence of its deepening and broadening of our relationships. But disruption is not necessarily destructive. Although the risks cannot be removed, they can be lessened. This occurs in ways that also enhance the value of solitude. The first constructive reaction to the problem is to recognize the condition of solitude. This obvious reaction is not easy. Solitude occurs often, sometimes in a very brief length of time, and it is frequently concealed. We need to become far more aware of our own experiences of solitude and those of others. The characteristics and disguises of solitude need to become familiar to us. Our usual perception of solitude includes only the extreme, either dramatic or traditional, forms that mask recognition of it as a basic element in our daily lives. The first task is, therefore, continually to point out experiences of solitude to ourselves and to others.

The second constructive reaction to the disruption of solitude is to grant permission to both ourselves and others for solitude. This means giving freedom for the many ways of being alone without being lonely, but most especially with acknowledgment that real solitude can contribute to relationship. Solitude is a triumph of both the individual will and the social will. One who seeks solitude and lives in solitude must have the confidence that this condition is of value to both self and others. The confidence is a consequence of previous and present relationships which grant the freedom to venture forth despite risks to the relationship. Permission is granted by parent to child, lover to lover, one generation to another, and by God to humankind (and, we hope, vice versa). So solitude is not only the recognition of relationship but also the consequence of it. This permission should be connected with our fuller awareness of the phenomenology of solitude. Our permission is not to occur only on rare occasions of extreme need, but to be as frequent as the condition itself. We are seeking and granting (or failing to grant) permission for solitude all the time. Failing to realize this, we only foster inflated needs that are likely to be more destructive than not.

The third constructive reaction involves a creative focus on the ritual support of solitude. Traditionally in many societies religion contained a wealth of ritual support. Retreats for individual and group, private meditation and prayer, and public worship—these provided established and approved ways of being alone or with others in the powerful condition of solitude. Community participation in ritual, we should realize, is not companionship any more than it is loneliness; it is attention to relationship. Contemporary society does not have so many approved rituals for this purpose, so we have been left to our own idiosyncratic devices. We cannot create new rituals by fiat, but there should be more acknowledgment of the need for ritual support of solitude. Such recognition would lessen disguised ritual and, consequently, confusion and deception. Shared recognition would offer the possibility of new rituals supported by society. Rather than engage in what would almost inevitably be judged as antisocial behavior, we could write about it. A superb example of solitude as ritual behavior is the experience of Kate Brown in *The Summer Before the Dark*.[52] Her reflective action and its dangers are clearly evident to the reader. Writing the novel may have served the function of ritual solitude for the author, Doris Lessing. To create and tell a story about such events has as powerful an effect without the damaging consequences to oneself and others as living out these events. If we cannot write, we can read. Much reading of poetry and fiction and much attendance in theater and cinema is ritual behavior. To read and become fully involved in *The Summer Before the Dark* can be, not blind engagement, reclusiveness, or narcissism, but a reflection in solitude. The challenge is to discover and explore these and all other ritual ways of recognizing relationship that could and do occur in our lives. Some of these relationships take place when we are alone, while others are really parallel solitude in which two or more of us are not really in companionate action although we are in each other's supportive presence. The possibilities for a creative response to the ritual needs of solitude are great because we have ignored them so fully.

In order to begin discovery and exploration of our own ritual support for solitude, we can consider these questions.

1. What are the formal customs of our society that you use most frequently? On what occasions are these customs used, and what is the power and danger involved?
2. What is an informal, individual custom of your own? On what occasion does it arise and what is the power and danger involved?
3. Recall an experience of solitude in which your "doing" with another person(s) was not companionship but ritual action.
4. How free do you feel to engage in solitude? Very. Fairly. Somewhat.
5. Who are the persons important to you for granting permission for your solitude?
6. Which of these persons grant you sufficient permission and which do not?
7. To what extent are you able to grant yourself permission for your solitude? A great extent. A fair extent. Somewhat.
8. What are the concerns that inhibit your granting permission for your solitude?

9. Who are the persons who might seek permission from you for solitude?
10. To what extent do you give permission to them? A great extent. A fair extent. Little.
11. What kinds of ritual support of solitude do you practice that might be new and useful to others?

## Conclusion

The mood of solitude tends to be most affirmative, so we have dwelt on the problems of this condition. We have difficulties entering it, staying in it, leaving it, and being disrupted by it. But we cannot eliminate it. Solitude's danger to self and society is the consequence of its power, and its power is a consequence of its necessity. Solitude rewards us with increased awareness of the depth and breadth of relationship.

Recall the three challenges of loneliness: actually to face our loneliness; to see both our separation and our search and work for balance between them; and to acknowledge the five realms of relationship, to experience and explore the breadth of our loneliness. Facing these challenges exposes us to the richness of loneliness, and to its irony when it occurs in the very midst of our relationships. The natural outcome of such fulsome awareness of our loneliness is movement into the condition of solitude. This shift happens when our recognition of relationship occurs. Full awareness of loneliness fosters a transcendence of it. So solitude is a continuation of this process of deepening and broadening relationship awareness.

Depth in solitude refers to our experience and acknowledgment of just how fundamental relationship per se is to us. We can live in many kinds of relationships for years without much awareness of them, just as infants and children do. In the adult years, we have opportunity and natural demand for conscious appreciation of this fundamental fact of life. It is recognition of how fully bound we are to the other, that we do not and cannot exist without the other, and that we find our fullest satisfaction in linking with the other. Full acknowledgment of this brute and glorious fact is no easy achievement. We may be inclined to place far more stress on independence, even to the extent of granting ourselves the illusion of absolute freedom to choose or reject relationship per se whatever the circumstances. Such beliefs can serve to support our frightening entries into the precariousness of adult responsibilities. But we come to see our humble captivity, to respect it, and to embrace it as a need that is quite beyond our control. Full experience of solitude grants us this depth of understanding of relationship, not just intellectual understanding, but a faith in how things "really" are. Paradoxically, it is just this depth experience of relationship that moves us out of solitude into companionship.

The outcome of our solitude is also increased breadth of relationship. We are free to extend relationship as much as we can, and this is our natural propensity—to seek new relational stimulation. The possibilities are endless. They occur both within our customary realms of relationship and within those we have previously ignored. If our social network has consisted primarily of associates on the job, then the possibility in solitude is the discovery and exploration of relationships in other groups. If we have found friendship primarily with a spouse, then the challenge is to extend the range to friendship with other people. Whatever our focus, there is room for expansion and the possibility for it. This includes the other realms which may be somewhat foreign to us. We can, in solitude, be surprised by an interest in the material realms through nature or art, the historical realm of the generations through interest in the forebears of our family, or an interest in the world as a whole probing of the meaning of life. Real solitude, then, does not dwell only on the familiar. It is a lively condition, full of surprises.

Solitude is awesome because recognition of relationship is a fundamental source of our faith, hope, and love—of our capacity to live. It is also awful because it challenges us to explore relationship without destroying it. But when the challenge is met, companionship is on the way. Solitude calls our attention to relationship so that we can move meaningfully from loneliness to companionship.

# Companionship

# CHAPTER IX

# *The Action*
# *of Companionship*

When we try to think about the action of relationship, we face the difficulty of trying to understand what is too fundamental to understand. A companion is one who is in company with us or accompanies us. What is said so simply does not appear to tell us much, but this generality and impreciseness is a value. It allows us to speak of lovers, friends, relatives, members of interest groups, as companions, regardless of all the real differences between such relationships. We could not so easily subsume all our human connections under the common understandings of love or friendship. Further, because of our special meanings for these two kinds of relationship, we do not easily use them in reference to dogs and paintings. Perhaps we are all too prone to think of the world, especially in the form of God, as a lover or friend. So, however vague, the word "companion" is useful because of its breadth of application.

Before we go further in recalling and expanding our understanding of relational action, we can begin deliberate exploration of our own experience of companionship. Take pencil and paper and write on top of the sheet: "My Own Companionship." Write a statement of no more than one hundred words on a personal experience of companionship. Tell the event in story form. Do not worry about spelling, grammar, or literary merit. Select an experience you would not mind sharing with anyone. Take ten minutes to do this. Do it now before reading any farther.

After you have committed this narrative to paper, respond to the following questions.

1. Who is your companion(s)?
2. To which one or more of the realms of individuals, groups, generations, things, and world does your companion belong?
3. What were the positive aspects of this event for you?
4. What were the positive aspects of this event for your companion?
5. What were the negative aspects of this event?
6. What were the characteristics of the mood that arose while you wrote your narrative?

You have now written three narratives, each illustrating your own experience with the fundamental conditions of relationship. Rereading the earlier two may help you reflect on how companionship differs from the other conditions. If you are in the company of others, these new stories should be shared and compared. What are the similarities and differences regarding the realms involved, the positive and negative aspects of the experience, and any other matters? And whether or not you are exploring with others, it would be useful for you to reflect on the mood involved in your own experience of companionship. Like loneliness and solitude, companionship is a complex condition, so your mood is likely to be a rich source of personal understanding. All this material can be related to the theory about companionship which follows.

### What Companionship Is: Collaboration and Empathy

Companionship occurs when we move from being an I-person to being a We-person. The movement results in an expanded ego, or, to use the more traditional metaphor, an expanded heart. The discovery of this occurs in solitude, but the doing of it is in companionship. At some point in our lives, probably in preadolescence, we discover that we can collaborate with another.[53] This is not just a matter of give-and-take according to rules, nor is it any partial loss of the self. Rather, we discover that someone is valuable to us and we are valuable to him or her. Therefore, we both enjoy modifying our behavior in ways that increase mutuality. This experience is extraordinarily affirmative. When we find someone valuable who also finds us valuable, we can conclude that we must actually be of value.[54] The movement from the I-person to the We-person is one into the experience of caring and being cared for in the most profound way. We say to ourselves, "Whatever is going on with me must be human and therefore to be cherished, as I can see that the same things go on in my friend."[55] Recall your relationships from around the age of eight and a half to ten or more. Did you have a "chum," a close friend, most likely of the same sex and nearly the same age, with whom you discovered an intimacy in which both you and your chum were expanded? If you did not have a chum, can you recall knowing that others did, and did you long for one? Try to remember. No doubt this will give rise to awareness of present chums or the lack of them. It can be useful to make a list of the persons with whom you have been chums in the past and with whom you are chums in the present. It is a reminder of those who have enabled us to see ourselves as We-persons, as valuable to ourselves and others.

A word that helps us understand this collaboration with another is "empathy." There are characteristics of this condition that we can see in ourselves.[56] The feelings of another become a part of our own feelings, so that we are not able to be indifferent to the other's happiness or sadness. We try to help the other just as we try to help ourselves, quite spontaneously. This is out of our control, maybe even to our dismay at times. Also, when in the presence of the other, more of us comes out into the open. We have the feeling that we are more alive, more in touch with ourselves, and more in touch with everything. In all these ways characteristic of empathy, we experience expansion of ego or heart. The two do not become one. Rather, each one becomes more than before. A love in which one loses one's heart is just that—loss of heart. A love in which one steal's another's heart is just that—theft. Empathy is about relationship, not union.

What is put so abstractly in terms of collaboration and empathy is illustrated by an event in the uncompleted novel *Absurd Friendship* by Jean-Paul Sartre. The hero is Brunet, a Communist Party leader in a Nazi prisoner-of-war camp. He has a friend in prison with him who has secretly left the Party and betrayed it. Others set out to kill his friend. Brunet cannot allow this and so engineers an escape for both of them. But their plan has been betrayed to the Germans. As they run away in a hail of bullets, the friend is shot. Brunet gathers him into his arms, and thinks:

> This absolute of suffering, no human victory will be able to efface it: it is the Party which drove him to his death; even if the U.S.S.R. gains, men are alone.

The story continues:

> Brunet . . . plunged his hand into the soiled hair of
> Vicarios. He cried out as if he could still save him
> from the horror, as if two lost men might be able, at
> the last minute, to conquer solitude: "The hell with
> the Party! You are my only friend."[57]

But his chum is already dead. Brunet cries out again: "My only
friend!" Then he rises and marches into the bullets of his enemies.
What is "absurd friendship" for an I-person is not so for a We-
person.

Companionship is defined abstractly by the ideas of collaboration
and empathy, and illustrated concretely by our stories of love and
friendship. Images may be more fundamental than either idea or
experience. We have referred to one image, the expanded heart.
Another is suggested by the term "companion" itself. It comes from
the Latin, being composed of terms for "together" and "bread," and
means breaking bread together. Sharing food in a meal is one of the
fundamental human activities, both an act for survival and an ultimate religious act in many traditions. Like sexual intercourse, breathing, and only a few other comparable actions, it is rich with associations and meanings at every level of individual and social and
religious existence. The breadth of being a companion is indicated,
for we do break bread with lovers, families, friends, associates, strangers, and even enemies. And we do so in relationship to animals and
to God as well. The act can be trivial or profound. Either or both
parties can have gathered and prepared the food. Each can feed
himself or herself, one can feed the other, or both can feed each other.
We can remember the feelings of our experience of eating to survive,
eating for physical satisfaction, and eating together for enjoying and
caring. What is companionship? Whatever is signified by the image
of a loaf of bread being broken by the hands of different persons.

Before we begin to think about the action of relationship in a more
precise way, it is appropriate for you to explore your own understanding of what companionship is. You have recorded an experience
of companionship and you have followed the above brief discussion
of its nature. Now you are to approach companionship as an image
and give your understanding of what companionship looks like to
you. Take another sheet of paper and write on top of it: "An Image
of Companionship." Now take pen, pencil, or, best, Magic Marker,

and draw an image of companionship—no words allowed. This is not a test of artistic ability. No image can be right or wrong. And whatever you draw will not be the only image you have. At another time, another image would appear. We all have a collection of images of companionship. So do not believe that what you draw will reveal all. The exercise should take only three minutes. You may think first and then draw, or you may just move the pen or marker on the paper first. If you sit there and no images come to mind, just start moving the implement on the paper and an image will appear. Remember to take no more than about three minutes. Careful thinking is neither required nor helpful. Just move your drawing implement on the paper. Do it now.

If you are alone, you might try to draw several more images, and, in addition, think of various images of companionship in paintings and in any of the literary arts that come to mind. The point is to collect a group of images significant for you. If you are in a group, the task is easy, as you are to share the images you have drawn in a "show-and-tell." Please note that we are not to give a psychological analysis of these images, but should say what we can about our own images and realize that there may be much about their meaning for us that we either do not choose to say to others or do not even know ourselves. In discussion with others or in reflection with ourselves, we can think about the similarities and differences in the images, what surprises us about them, and what understandings of companionship are suggested by them. My assumption is that our understanding and action are highly influenced by the images from within us, as much, if not more, than by our verbal definitions and narratives. The images can function primarily to underscore what our conscious position about companionship is, but they are just as likely to reveal an equally real position that adds to the conscious one. If your own conscious understanding seems quite different from what is suggested by your nonverbal image, you have a fine opportunity to see what each adds to the other and so increase your comprehension of how you see companionship in your life. Now, as the last stage of reflection on the image, you can relate it to the theory given about movement from an I-person to a We-person, collaboration and empathy. How are these ideas supported, developed, and/or challenged by your image? And what other ideas are suggested by your image? Answering these questions gives you fuller understanding of companionship in general and of your own companionship specifically.

### Demonstrating Relationship

Companionship is relational action. Relationship is a process in which certain things have to happen in order for the process to continue—demonstrating, maintaining, and developing. They do not guarantee continuance, indeed they may bring it to an end. But companionship still requires these three elements if it is to occur.

The element of demonstrating relationship is obvious, although we are sometimes forgetful about it. Companionship is being with a person or thing. It differs from solitude, in which relationship is recognized but not demonstrated. To recognize that a relationship exists is not the same as saying hello. Some long-term companions may forget to say hello. Action on the recognition is forgotten. But tenderness and affection cannot be superseded. Old chums of various kinds need such reminders. New chums may have problems also. Our new relationships recall previous experiences with all their limitations, and so give rise to fear, hate, or guilt. There must be enough toleration of such feelings in ourselves and in others so that demonstrating can occur and continue nevertheless. We all have some need to repudiate our need for tenderness in an attempt to protect our self-esteem. Tolerance for this is essential, but only so far as not to preclude some affectional action. The challenge is to demonstrate tenderness with some humble awareness of how scared we can be and usually are.

Another danger is to make too much of demonstrating as a peak experience more significant than the other elements of maintaining and developing. Recall two young friends discovering that they can share a discourse about the self and not be ridiculed; two old friends meeting after years of separation and realizing that they are as close as they ever were; and two lovers at the moment of declaring their surprising mutual love. These are extraordinary moments of demonstrating. It is understandable that we use them as symbols of the whole relational process. But reduction of relationship to such moments is destructive. There are also the preludes and postludes. And there are different and equal satisfactions in the other elements. To limit love to such a peak experience of the moment of mutual declaration is as narrow and misguided as to limit sexual intercourse to the moment of orgasm. And the first moments of love contain much foolishness from the perspectives of the other components of relationship. There is instant sex, but not instant companionship. Demonstration should be neither ignored nor made too much of.

Consider now your own experience with demonstrating relationship.

1. Recall an example of demonstrating relationship from your own experience. Note it briefly and concretely.
2. Recall the companionship narrative you wrote and the image you drew. Note the demonstrating present in them, if any.
3. To what extent and in what way did these experiences of demonstrating satisfy you?
4. What difficulties did you have with the demonstrating in these experiences?

### Developing Relationship

Companionship is usually developing and never at a permanent standstill. But not all relationships are companionships. Developing is not an issue, for example, when the concern is validation of sexual performance in adolescent exploits. The goal in this case is integration of sexual intercourse into one's consciousness, not the relationship between two people. Other relationships may be longer and deeper, but serve some emergency purpose. The connection of a patient and a crisis-oriented psychotherapist may be highly passionate, but serve only a specific purpose which is soon outgrown, and the relationship develops only by coming to an end. Companionship is different in that growth is expected, and expected to be mutual. Each person is expected to grow, and the relationship itself is expected to grow.

The goal of development is mutuality and this depends on some amount of similarity. Ideally, two persons need only reciprocity of interest in each other.[58] We value helping the other person, understanding and accepting the other, and general trustworthiness. But our actual relationships seem to depend more on similarity—shared experience in past and present, ease of communication, having similar behavior and shared interests, ideas, and values. Further, the similarity between two persons should include a similarity in developmental paths.[59] It is fashionable for some to make much of the value of people being opposites in order to complement each other. Such an approach does not fit what we know. It is likely that the opposites observed in companions are of minor significance to them, whereas the more crucial similarities are overlooked. Have you ever been quite lacking in comprehension of a loved one's cherished concern or major project? No degree of relaxed permissiveness can effectively counter our puzzlement. It suggests that something is wrong in us, in the other, or in the relationship. So we have an ideal of helping, understanding, and trusting another, but this depends markedly upon a similarity between us, especially in our developmental paths.

The mutuality we seek involves using one another. Our relationships are strong when we can see, accept, and share the necessities for the growth of our partner.[60] We are to be committed to the growth of the other as well as of ourselves. The point needs to be put most directly: our deepest connections are to the persons who help us move ahead in our living. However crass it may sound when we speak of this, we employ each other for our own benefit. No human relations piety should be allowed to obscure this truth. Manipulation of another for one's own ends is not involved. Rather, there is an open understanding that one person asks for help, receives it, and enjoys receiving from the other. The other enjoys being used. The theme is mutual employment and the enjoyment of employing and being employed. Not to acknowledge such employment is silly and not to have it is sad. The gratification to companions for this using and being used for developing is enormous.

Developing makes companionship a lively condition. Crises are inevitable. It challenges the status quo, however satisfactory it might be. It awakens new possibilities that can frighten either party. Or there can be negative feelings connected with old possibilities that were awakened in the past. Also, the kind of growth stimulated in another by one partner may not be an area of the other's crucial concern. This newness of concern can confront the partner with matters that are incomprehensible. More than this, the new issues may be precisely what the partner cannot deal with at all and needs to ignore at present. Further, development concerns maturity. We are not fully grown up in all areas of our lives and have the need to work out juvenile and adolescent concerns under the guise and disguise of mature relationship. So it is as children and adolescents that we can relate to each other. This can satisfy and foster belated development, especially if the partners understand their actual needs and do not pretend that they are otherwise. It is the pretense of mature companionship that is likely to endanger the relationship more than the typical immature needs per se. All the above are just some of the crises that can occur because of developing in companionship.[61]

Companionship is risky. Developing is change, and change can diminish the similarity that supports companionship. It can so separate the companions that the relationship ends. This accounts for the existence of some relationships that try to continue without growth or any kind of change at all. But this is likely to occur despite our attempts at stability because people and environments do change. Further, attempts at covering up change are not likely to be successful for long. Deterioration of relationship is caused equally by puzzlement over change or by lack of change. But these crises that are due to developing can be overcome and serve as spurs for more developing of relationship if we and our partners are interested and capable, able, and willing to express tenderness, and are dedicated to developing. Crises are opportunities as much as they are problems. They are highly demanding, but they make it clear that we do not just need similarity and mutual employment but that we also need and enjoy developing itself.

Consider now your own experience with developing relationship.

1. Recall an example of developing relationship from your own experience. Note it briefly and concretely.
2. Recall the companionship narrative you wrote and the image you drew. Note the developing present in them, if any.
3. To what extent and in what way did these experiences of developing satisfy you?
4. What difficulties did you have with developing in these experiences?

## Maintaining Relationship

"Maintaining" is an unimpressive term for what seems a dreary aspect of companionship. But consider what the absence of such activity would be like. All action would be demonstrating affection or developing the self, the other, and relationship per se. This would be lively, so much so that we would become exhausted by such continual feeling of passion and continual work at development. Compulsive action in love and friendship may be beneficial for adolescents who are also allowed to sleep a lot and recover from the frenzy, but the rest of us do not have this luxury. Chronic passion and improvement can become false, and we end up lying to ourselves and others. Even if this does not happen, it is possible for continual action of this sort to bore the partner. Maintenance action provides relief.

But maintaining is not as dreary as it sounds. It is action that supports the connection. An example is joint action on accepted responsibilities. Two parents do something together with or about their child, or two friends work together on a community committee. Such action is neither demonstrating nor developing necessarily, but is a maintaining of the relationship. A couple have regular habits of seeing a movie together on Friday nights, or of doing housework together, or even just sitting down and sharing sections of the newspaper. There are extraordinarily good times of ease and comfort that occur in this maintaining action. The satisfaction of having another person around can itself be quite strong. Physical presence is a form of maintaining. Unfortunately for our understanding, maintaining tends to be unnoticed except in its absence. What is missed by us when we are lonely? Probably not the great passion or the developmental challenges, but the lowly maintaining behavior, undramatic though it is. Consider two persons in bed together. There is demonstrating by means of sexual intercourse, and developing by means of occasions of long, probing discussion. Are these missed most? It is possible, but the other hours spent in bed together with neither great sex nor discussion may be profoundly mourned. It is the saying of good night, the issue of who turns off the light or sets the alarm, or the conflict over how high the window should be raised, and just the breathing and shifting of the body nearby—this is what is missed. Such behavior really does maintain our relationships. Further, what works this way is enjoyable. Even our arguments and all-out battles can have a maintaining aspect in which our enjoyment, however covert it might be, is major. We have a mass of largely unnoticed behavior which supports and pleases us and our companions. Such action is notable for its comfort. Neither demonstrating nor developing are necessarily comfortable. They can be exciting, but not really comforting. Maintaining behavior is a kind of cuddling. It need not be physical, as there is a psychosocial cuddling that comforts as well.

After we have made a place for routine behavior, it is appropriate to say that a relationship with only cuddling becomes smug, complacent, and boring. Human beings do not seek only to make themselves secure and content in relationship. The urge to novelty will tend to assert itself and will comment on the limitations of the routine. A chronic respite from demonstrating and/or developing is destructive. Even so, we should not use this danger as a way of ignoring the functional value and delights of maintaining relationships.

Consider now your own experience with maintaining relationship.

1. Recall an example of maintaining relationship from your own experience. Note it briefly and concretely.
2. Recall the companionship narrative you wrote and the image you drew. Note the maintaining present in them, if any.
3. To what extent and in what way did these experiences of maintaining satisfy you?
4. What difficulties did you have with maintaining in these experiences?

### Conclusion

Companionship is relational action, not the search for or recognition of relationship, but the actual action of it. This action is so fundamental that it is difficult to understand except by the use of metaphors such as breaking bread together or expanding the heart. But the basic conclusion of this chapter is that the action consists of three activities—demonstrating, developing, and maintaining—which are equally necessary for relationship to be and continue. The following questions offer us some directions for exploring our own experience of companionship further.

1. Which of the three elements of companionship do you tend to focus on?
2. Which of the three do you tend to ignore?
3. Which of the three is the most comfortable for you? Indicate why.
4. Which of the three is the most difficult for you? Indicate why.
5. Recall an experience when you and a companion had a focus on a different one of the three elements at the same time. How did the two of you handle this difference?
6. Recall a relationship in which each of you habitually focused on a different one of the three elements. How did the two of you handle this difference?

We are accustomed to think of our companions as being other individuals—friends, lovers, relatives, neighbors, colleagues, or whatever. But this typical focus is quite narrow and restrictive. Just as our loneliness is too small and our solitude too unsurprising, so also is our companionship. Beyond individuals are groups, different cultures, generations, and the whole human race. And beyond people are material objects and the world as a whole. There are innumerable ways in which the heart can be expanded, and these possible companionships consist of demonstrating, developing, and maintaining. What is the possible and appropriate developing in a relationship between us and an inanimate object? What are the workings of maintaining in our relationship to God? What is demonstration of affection for a past generation and its living members? Such questions are without end for us if we are open to explore our companionships more broadly. The following questions are a guide.

1. Recall an experience of companionship in the realm of groups. Which elements of companionship were focused on, ignored, most comfortable, most difficult, and why?
2. Recall an experience of companionship in the realm of the generations. Which elements of companionship were focused on, ignored, most comfortable, most difficult, and why?
3. Recall an experience of companionship in the realm of things. Which elements of companionship were focused on, ignored, most comfortable, most difficult, and why?
4. Recall an experience of companionship in the realm of the world as a whole. Which elements of companionship were focused on, ignored, most comfortable, and most difficult, and why?

In addition to the above, you can explore timing, those occasions in which these companions and you differ in the need for, and expectation of, demonstrating, developing, and maintaining. It is also possible that some of our learning about companionship in these other realms will inform us about what we are doing with individual human beings. Companionship has connotations of travel. It is movement, not physically or even mentally only, but relational movement. It is a movement of the ego in expanding. Such an ego will always have questions, always want to know: "With whom and with what and in what ways can I be a companion?"

# CHAPTER X

# Loneliness, Solitude, and Companionship

Searching, meeting, and accompanying are the three conditions in all our relationships. Loneliness is our experience of separation from and search for relationship. Solitude is our experience of recognition—discovery and exploration—of relationship. Companionship is the demonstrating, maintaining, and developing of relationship. This summary of what we have been exploring is a reminder that the conditions are connected. The purpose of this chapter is to describe these connections and present them as our ways of living in relationships. The problems and possibilities we encounter are depicted by the circle of conditions—by an image of a circle composed of double-headed arrows connecting three smaller circles.

## Equal Value

The first theme is given simply and briefly, some of the implications becoming clear only during discussion of the other conditions. The three small circles in the image are equal in size and this represents the theme that one condition is as useful to us as another. We have already established the value of the separation and search of loneliness despite the typically negative feeling about this experience, the value of the discovery and exploration of relationship in the aloneness of solitude despite its distance from concrete relationship, and, of course, the value of companionship is all too blindly accepted without an understanding of its limitations. So this theme of equality is a summary of our previous discussion of the functions of the conditions. All serve the cause of relationship.

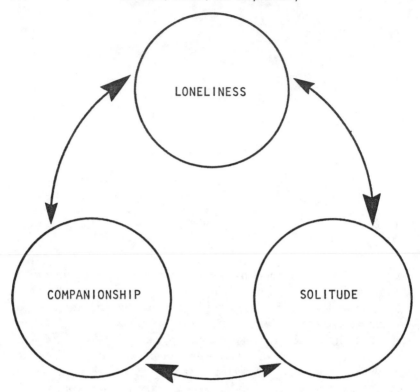

It is one thing to reach this intellectual conclusion and quite another to act upon it and live accordingly. It means that there are
occasions during our days, months, or years when any one condition
can be most valuable and should be encouraged. This applies, not just
to time periods, but to any specific relationship as well. The point is
that no relationship is without a need for each of the conditions. For
example, there is an appropriate time to search for the world as a
whole, so loneliness in the absence of God can be constructive of
relationship. There is an appropriate time for developing a relationship with a pet animal, because both it and we change and because
we have very likely ignored the possibilities of growth in such a
relationship, being rather unimaginative, even unfair, to both the
animal and ourselves. And there is an appropriate time for distance
from our family or colleagues, so that recognition of the connections
can be renewed. The difficulties raised by the point of view are
obvious. We may need to be in a different condition than we wish

to remain in, or we may be in the appropriate condition and yet want to get out of it. Certainly we can recall times of conscious disagreement with the condition pressing in upon us. Some of this disagreement may have been unwise. We do not always want company after experiencing the delights of solitude, and surely we are not inclined to welcome loneliness, although some of us are disinclined to leave loneliness too, considering it too dangerous to leave. Further, the timing between ourselves and others may be off, the condition useful for one person being different from the condition useful for another. We have probably worked in and for a group and experienced times when we needed demonstration of the group's concern for us, but the group needed primarily to distance itself from individual members and explore itself as a group per se in solitude. These and other difficulties indicate that our tolerance for equality in value of the three conditions is likely to be hard to come by. Once it no longer flies in the face of our judgment, we still have work to do in accepting and then using the conditions of relationship.

This fundamental point is so simple, and possibly deceptively so, that some clear attention to our own experience is advisable.

1. Recall an experience in which you were in one of the conditions appropriately, but did not wish to be, and had great difficulty in accepting it.
2. Recall an experience in which it would have been appropriate for you to move from one condition to another, but you did not wish to, and had great difficulty in doing so.
3. Recall an experience in which the condition appropriate for you and the one appropriate for another differed. Note both the occasion and the consequences.

### Necessary Movement

The second theme concerning the circle of conditions is the necessity of movement. If the three conditions are equal in value and only one can occur at a time, then movement is required. Each points and leads us beyond itself. Therefore, no condition is a final state, but appears again and again in any relationship. It is both necessary and to our advantage to move. Since we are free to resist, some discussion of the acceptance of movement is appropriate.

The negative term that is pertinent here is "chronic." Except under the most rare circumstances, chronic loneliness is avoidable. We who maintain it are most likely seeking to protect ourselves by avoiding relationship. Chronic loneliness preserves self-esteem at the cost of connectedness. Chronic solitude is not better, although the mood enveloping it is more affirmative. This also is flight from the action of relationship, another way of protecting ourselves from risk. Chronic companionship is the most pernicious of these attempts to avoid vulnerability. Our tendency is to see companionship as the end goal. We do not baldly proclaim that "they married and lived happily ever after," but much of our behavior suggests that this belief remains. We relax considerably when the goal of companionship is reached in our lives. When we do not relax, but work and play in order that the relationship may develop, we set a new goal of deeper mutuality. This is a legitimate goal, but the fact that such valid attention to relationship can stop companionship and return us to loneliness comes as a shock—as life's foul play. Intellectually, we may accept the fact that movement from companionship to loneliness must occur. Development of ourselves or of the relationship itself creates something new: this strangeness calls for a different relationship, and the uncertainty involved produces loneliness. But this is very difficult to accept emotionally. So we may well affirm that none of these three conditions should be chronic, but we are most likely to hope to the contrary and especially to hope that companionship might be an exception.

Our relationships are processes of continual change. The movement from companionship into loneliness is difficult when required by outer circumstances such as the death of a loved one. Perhaps it is even more difficult when required by inner circumstances such as developmental change. This is so because we perceive companionship as stable. Our need to have such a perception is very strong. But it is also very easy to fulfill the need, because we integrate many little changes that appear over a length of time into an overall pattern without awareness that the changes occur. So change, which is happening all the time, is not seen. Then we can be shocked when drastic change breaks through to our consciousness. At worst, we are immobilized by the discovery of extreme change. But, at best, we become reacquainted with the fact of continual change in relationships.

The necessary movement in relationship can be used when it becomes both present in and accepted by the consciousness. We are not free to eliminate change, although we are free to deny it, retard or hasten it, and modify it in other ways. Best of all, we are free to use movement in relationship between two persons. At some point we realize that we are lonely. To accept and flow with this change is to affirm that our loneliness is real—that the separation from our loved one is real and that our search for some kind of reconnection is real. We can explore the cause of separation—role of our partner, our self, difficulties in us and/or society that are avoidable, and the fact of existential separateness as the human condition. Such examination of the change in our relationship can prevent our all too easy blame of self or loved one, our too easy flight to relationship with a different partner, and our too easy denial of loneliness itself. Further, our examination can ferret out those aspects of the relationship which can be changed and those which cannot and which must be accepted as part of the arrangement. All this leads to a search that can be both realistic and optimistic, rather than to one that is covert, or superficial, or pessimistic. Our affirmation of movement from the companionship of love to loneliness is a reaction of realistic hope which counteracts our tendency both to deny and to despair over loneliness and so to slowly kill the collaboration and empathy that are our natural potential. Acting on our freedom to use necessary change is encouraging.

We need to reflect on the use of necessary movement in friendship also. Only rather abrupt shifts remind us of the value of our friends. When one of them changes residence, dies, or breaks up the relationship—by lack of interest or betrayal—we wake up a little into loneliness. And our questions to ourselves about friendship are frightening. It is difficult to ask ourselves truly and concretely, "How many friends do I have?" More difficult to ask is, "How many of these friends are really close friends rather than just associates and acquaintances?" Perhaps the most difficult of all is to ask, "Just how close is my closest friend?" We are likely to flee these troubling questions. We may say to ourselves that close friendship is not really possible, people are only in love or in association with others, so friendship does not really exist. We can maintain old friendships with those who are at a distance and rarely come into our lives anymore. We can substitute work in groups, civic committees, or volunteer organizations for friendship. Or we can pay for membership in individual or group therapy as a way of buying into friendship without acknowledging it. But if we acknowledge the separation, our search can occur and be creative. To look at our own friendship patterns involves seeing our acquaintances, associates, friends, closest friends, and love relationships. In selecting our actual friends out of this large number of relationships, we then become aware of the difficulty of establishing, maintaining, and developing friendships, of the degree of mutual affirmation and validation present, of the amount of honesty and tenderness, of the degree of differences and similarities in commonality and values, and of the paradoxical experiences of precariousness and ultimate meaningfulness attached to the relationships. Probing such concerns in just a few relationships gives us much to reflect on. It also increases our loneliness, but it can provide the tolerance, patience, and determination necessary for renewal and establishment of new friendship. That is, our search can be more realistic and hopeful. Acting on our freedom to use necessary change is encouraging.

The necessity of movement from one condition to another and our freedom to use it creatively applies to all three conditions of relationship. Most of us may be tempted to remain in companionship, but this is not true of us all. We have observed that solitude is preferable for some of us who may or may not acknowledge it. And the same is true even for loneliness, the search being more restful and/or safe than the meeting of solitude or the accompanying of companionship. We can deceive ourselves and others all too easily on this matter. Some of us may believe that we either seek or are in companionship when we really are in the reflective distance of solitude and want to stay there. Others of us may believe that we want to meet and accompany another, but are using self-pity to avoid confession of contentment with loneliness. In sum, it would be a mistake to assume automatically that all of us are tempted primarily toward chronic residence in companionship.

We need to consider our movement in all five realms of relationship also. Surely it is dangerous to be comfortable with our companionship with the past generation. An older adolescent's connection with parents and their generation will serve for a while, but changes in the person and in the generation also will prompt loneliness and the possibility of a new relationship. When this does not happen, neither party is served and society is neither supported nor improved. Such rigidities can affect us at all stages in life: an older generation refusing to acknowledge the new possibilities and the younger one refusing to acknowledge the contribution of the old realities. Our relational movement is just as necessary with objects. Cats, flowers, vases, mountain paths, and old trinkets can be sought in loneliness, but also need to be recognized in solitude and accompanied in companionship. Some of us may not search enough, while others may not meet or accompany enough. A stored trinket from the distant past needs to be taken out, dusted, and shown. A cat in a large family of humans needs to be allowed some aloneness. Some music should be played rarely so as not to become cheapened by familiarity even though its absence makes us lonely. Finally, with the world as a whole we may have occasion to make good use of movement from one condition to another. Both parties need loneliness and solitude at times, not just companionship. Our typical demand for God to be continually on call is reminiscent of the demand of a child for its parent, and is not characteristic of a mature relationship that encourages the other to both aloneness and other relationships. And we need more toleration, perhaps, for our own loneliness in relationship to the world as a whole; we need to acknowledge it, let it expand in us without grabbing for a quick affair with God.

If we do assume that movement is necessary and that we have real freedom to use it creatively with regard to the three conditions and the five realms, then we have a rich situation to explore in ourselves. There are a great many options that we may be using. We may be tempted differently in different realms, defaulting in a variety of ways. In one realm, for example, with objects of the natural world, we may chronically exist in companionship while residing in solitude with regard to humans and in loneliness regarding the world as a whole. All three realms are deprived by these limitations, and so are we deprived in all these relationships. So we should look carefully and fully into all the possible combinations of condition and realm that might be occurring in our relationships.

This discussion has been a reminder of the obvious fact that, if all three conditions are equal in value, there must be movement from one to another. Rest in loneliness ends in apathy, rest in solitude ends in stupor, and rest in companionship ends in boring routine. To help our awareness of this necessary movement here are some questions to consider.

1. Which of the three conditions of relationship are you most accepting of?
2. Which condition are you least accepting of?
3. Which condition is most prevalent in your present life?

4. Which condition has been most prevalent in your life as a whole?
5. In which condition might you be most likely to reside chronically in the future?
6. Indicate what you might gain from being in this possible chronic condition.
7. Indicate what you might lose from being in this possible chronic condition.
8. Which condition has been most prevalent in your life in each of the realms of relationship? Individual. Group. Generations. Things. World.

## *Directions*

The third theme on the circle of conditions is about the direction of movement. The basic direction has been implied by the order of presenting the conditions in this book. Somehow we find ourselves tumbled into loneliness. It is this condition we are likely to be aware of first rather than companionship because we take the latter for granted and become conscious of relationship through its loss. Then thorough separation and search prompts movement into solitude. The recognition of relationship through discovery and exploration prompts movement into companionship. Finally, the demonstrating, maintaining, and especially the developing aspects of companionship prompt movement into loneliness. The cycle repeats itself again and again in any specific relationship. Searching, meeting, and accompanying is a succession like other processes of nature that are a given with which we have to deal. However, natural events and human freedom combine to create other directions of movement. The image of the circle of conditions shows three possibilities. The large points on the arrows suggest the basic clockwise movement from companionship to loneliness to solitude and back to companionship. The smaller points on the opposite ends of the arrows suggest two other possibilities—oscillation and counterclockwise movement.

The first possibility is a movement back and forth between any two conditions. This can be helpful, or at least neutral, but a chronic oscillation can damage and lead to loss of relationship. Consider our movement between loneliness and solitude. This is without the action of relationship. Because we do not have the experience of the demonstrating, maintaining, and developing of relationship, we are led to apathy in alternation with stupor or narcissistic self-regard. We yearn for connection and find it only in fantasy. After building and dwelling in illusionary worlds of relationship for a while, the possibility of real companionship and actual contact with any person or object becomes a threat to the false world and is warded off. When we experience this oscillation in our relationships with individuals, we can sometimes see that we have isolated ourselves. Perhaps we do it just as often with groups, generations, objects, and the world as a whole, but other individuals let us know we are in such a trap, whereas nature, for example, leaves it up to us to find out. Probably we need to be more responsible to the signals from groups and the generations that we are moving between loneliness and solitude only, but it is up to us to awaken to our lack of companionship with things and with the world as a whole.

Another possibility is oscillation between solitude and companionship. This too may be useful, or at least neutral. There are times when we need to step back to examine a relationship by means of solitude. But a chronic alternation is another matter. Being without the separation and search of loneliness, we are led eventually to a stagnant and boring routine. The companionship is maintained and dwelt upon, but safety is the goal. Our relationship remains as a comfort, devoid of stimulation and challenge. This may appeal to us, openly or covertly, but it is irresponsible toward relational possibility. We can find ourselves yearning for this peace with lovers, friends, families, and relatives. But we are reminded of its limitations by the actual changes and demands of these intimates. If we are alert to the other realms, we will get the same message of change and threat of change. The problem for some of us is that we make a sly bargain with fate that we will be spared upheaval, a superstitious arrangement that the bars of our crib will not be broken.

The third option is to oscillate between companionship and loneliness. When we lack real recognition of relationship—both discovery and exploration—in solitude, our movement becomes a frightening and frenzied activity of shallow relationships and perpetual search in which we flit from one relationship to another in the instant "intimacy" of the desperate. Or we simply drive our companion crazy by our constant fussing with the relationship. Relations are casual, superficial, and without satisfaction, even though there is a terribly "serious" focus on the subject. Both self and other are manipulated for the sake of semblance of relationship. What we do with individuals in this manner, we do with groups, things, and gods. Some of us are busily joining and leaving community groups. Others of us are visiting thing after thing on vacations—sight-seeing—or buying thing after thing which are all appreciated for a period and then cast aside. And still others of us are spiritual shoppers who try on ultimate companions one after another, collecting idols continually. There are realms of relationship in which we probably need to become more reflective so that actual meeting can occur.

These three kinds of oscillation occur over and over again in our lives. They are not unnatural and dysfunctional unless they become chronic. Without companionship, there is isolation in illusion. Without loneliness, there is isolation in stagnation. Without solitude, there is isolation in manipulation. So our chronic oscillation wounds us just as much as our chronic attachment to a condition. Our movement has to both occur and be comprehensive, covering all three conditions.

Rather than oscillation, there can be a counterclockwise movement between the three conditions. This is a rare occurrence as a permanent pattern. In companionship, we can experience developments that prompt the distance of reflection in solitude. Our solitude, most naturally, moves us back into companionship, but it can break down into loneliness instead, our recognition of the relationship growing into new awareness of its limitations. So our loneliness can occur out of our solitude and this can prompt us to make a quick leap into companionship. This counterclockwise motion is too anxiety-provoking to last for very long. What is so lacking in satisfaction and threatening in meaning breaks up into any of the three possible oscillations or comes to an end by resting in just one of the conditions. But although this process is not often chronic, we do experience it. Perhaps what we sometimes believe to be an awful condition of loneliness is not that at all, but this countermovement through all three conditions that escalates our uncertainty to a pitch we cannot endure. Extreme loneliness includes some assurance of stability, no matter how negative it is. What we cannot tolerate is the change that occurs in the countermovement. Try to recall those occasions in which you found yourself plummeting downward in a spiral of this sort. Our memories of these spirals may be sufficient to increase our respect for our oscillations and chronic restings.

The basic conclusion is that our natural tendency is for a clockwise movement, although our circumstances and individual freedom allow for the rest stops, oscillations, and reverse directions. It is likely that each of us has experienced all the different movements in some or all of the different realms.

1. Recall an experience, whether short or long in duration, in which you moved through all three conditions in the natural order, beginning with any one of the three and arriving back at it again.
2. Recall an experience of oscillation between loneliness and solitude.
3. Recall an experience of oscillation between solitude and companionship.
4. Recall an experience of oscillation between companionship and loneliness.
5. Which of these three oscillations is the most typical in your life? Loneliness–solitude. Solitude–companionship. Companionship–loneliness.
6. Recall an experience of counterclockwise movement through the three conditions.

### Conclusion

The three themes suggested by the image of the circle of conditions are summarized by the observation that each condition is between the other two. This simple fact cannot be overstressed because of its bearing on our realism and hope. If we are lonely, it means that we have been in companionship and will come to a recognition of relationship in solitude. If we are in solitude, it means that we have been lonely and will enter into companionship. And if we are in companionship, we will become lonely. Each condition is an in-between state. Our awareness and acceptance of this grants us admission to the humbling and saving reality of relationship.

This image of the circle of conditions is a two-dimensional version of what can be a three-dimensional reality. Our relationships can and should be, not circles, but spirals. The spiral suggests our experience of growth. Ideally, we do not just go round and round in a two-dimensional circle from condition to condition with no real change, experiencing each condition the same way each time. This would be a situation of no growth. Rather, we have ups and downs, both loss and gain in understanding and behavior concerning the relationship. Movement from companionship to loneliness can be a fall, a walk on a level plain, or an ascent. Coming to a chronic rest would be a fall, oscillating between companionship and loneliness would most likely be a level walk for a while, but moving clockwise is quite naturally an ascent. In this three-dimensional movement, we enter each condition with the possibility of a richer awareness than before and a greater capacity to use the condition creatively. Actually our spirals dip downward, go along levelly, and ascend in most erratic paths. We move in crazy, mixed-up spirals at best. Add to this our rest stops, oscillations, and reverses, and we have a most lively pattern which can be charted for our significant relationships. It would take considerable time and thought to chart a long relationship in a manner that accounted for the major movements involved. Easier, and still useful, is to outline the basic spiral effect in a specific relationship. Do so as a conclusion to this chapter.

> Recall an experience of spiraling through the three
> conditions wherein growth occurred and a return to
> a previous condition on a new level.

# CHAPTER XI

# *Welcoming Strangers*

I hope you have already been surprised at strangeness in yourself, in others, and in your relationships. But the strangeness is more fundamental to our subject than this. Our loneliness can be followed by solitude and our solitude by companionship, but we know that this is not inevitable. Our egos have been enlarged, but only to a point. We are inclined to rest in exclusiveness. We are hampered by our inability to tolerate and welcome the strange, and our inability hampers others. Relationship is life and to decline it is death. Our exclusiveness kills. Moreover, relationship is always with the strange, so welcoming strangers is our only possibility. We explore this theme by first stating it more fully, and then applying it to our relationships with relatives and neighbors and other strangers.

## *Welcoming Strangers*

On those rare occasions when we look beyond ourselves fully, what we see and what sees us is vast and alien. Consider all who differ from what is familiar to us in race, class, sex and sexual preference, custom, ideology, generation, and so forth. The amount of strangeness is enormous. Most people in the world are very different from any one of us. The generations are also extensive, going back and back and back. This great majority is strange to us. The material world is mostly strange, since the vast bulk of it is quite unfamiliar to us other than by hearsay. The world as a whole is, of course, totally different from the small, comfortable world of our daily life of work

and play. People, things, and life itself are strange. It all looks at us
and seeks our returning looks. But it is too much for us to see, so we
do not see. That is, our world looks familiar to us; we do not see what
does not fit in. When we are forced to see what does not fit, we try
to make it fit at nearly any cost, including destruction of the unfitta-
ble. Rather than welcome, we wound. So the problem of exclusiveness is large in scale. It is not just a personal issue, but a social, indeed
a life, issue. Revelation of relationship is a revelation of responsibility. We are to welcome the strange.

The image of the circle of conditions of relationship has been
presented as a two-dimensional version of a three-dimensional reality. This spiral represents growth in old relationships and growth in
the development of new relationships. Therefore the spiral movement is the welcoming of strangers. The fundamental observation is
that welcoming the strange begins at home. Moving through the
three conditions is also a dual movement. We move from the familiar
to the strange and back again, from the common to the alien and back
again, from the satisfying to the stimulating and back again, and from
the comfortable to the frightening and back again. When a relationship is progressing—ascending in the spiral—we know our friend or
lover as a stranger. When a relationship is reduced to a circle and
from a circle to a dot, then we are only oscillating or resting, avoiding
the strangeness that we meet in the familiar relationship. Intimate
relationships fail because we cannot tolerate the strange, let alone
welcome it. Progress in an old relationship is progress in welcoming
the strange.

The second observation is that there can be progress in the development of new relationships. The spiral can not only ascend but also
increase in size, referring to ever-increasing numbers of relationships.
Ideally, the image grows in size and we establish more and more
relationships throughout our lives. The possibilities are endless, but
we often prefer not to have it so. Openness to the possibility of new
relationships is highly dependent on the dynamics of those we already have. If we find our friends and loved ones difficult and frightening, we will not be open to the previously unknown strangers. But
if the spiral movement is clearly established, we will have experienced the new in the old relationships sufficiently to have the
courage and interest to experience the old in the new. It is natural for
us to seek novelty and stimulation as well as satisfaction. Rejection
of novelty is abnormal, a consequence of our difficulty with it in the

familiar. So it is natural that the spiral should increase as our relationships broaden.

Welcoming the strange usually begins with the familiar. This
means two things: that a growing relationship with a lover or friend
involves welcoming the strange; and that welcoming the strange in
the familiar relationships enables us to welcome the strange in the
new and unfamiliar. However, these observations reflect only the
most common processes. Some of us may be most familiar, not with
friends and/or lovers, but with companions from other realms. And
some of us may find that welcoming of real strangers assists our
welcoming of the strange in our familiar relationships. So we should
state the two principles more generally: (1) a growing companionship
of any kind involves welcoming the strange; and (2) welcoming the
strange in any relationship, familiar or unfamiliar in nature, may help
us to welcome the strange in another relationship. But this issue is
one we handle badly, the spiral becoming a circle and the circle
shrinking to a point. The least we can do is not deceive ourselves. If
we are rejecting strangers whom we do not know, probably also we
are rejecting those strangers we do know, rejecting the strange in our
closest established relationships. And if our friend or lover rejects
strangers, most likely he or she is also rejecting the strange in us (no
small part of our personhood). If this is the least we can do, perhaps
the most we can do is to be surprised and enjoy it. Loneliness, solitude, and companionship are conditions in which we are surprised by
the strange. Whenever we are surprised in a relationship, we should
be thankful. It means that we are alive, are related, and can be even
more deeply and broadly related. It is strangeness that keeps us
moving in our relationships. Welcoming strangers and being welcomed by strangers is giving life to one another.

At the end of the last chapter, you were asked to recall an experience of spiraling through the three conditions wherein growth occurred and a return to a previous condition happened on a new level.
It is appropriate to consider such experiences as revelation of the
strange.

1. Recall a strange and alien aspect in a companion.
2. What was your response to the strangeness?
3. What do you believe your companion found to be strange in
   you?
4. What was your companion's response to your strangeness?

5. Recall the experience of spiraling you noted at the end of the previous chapter. What was the strangeness involved and what was your response to it?

## Relatives and Neighbors

Distinctions made between love and friendship are not especially convincing, because both are fundamentally becoming a We-person. We change our terms to fit with individual, social, and cultural understandings of differences that are rather minute. There are two ways in which these two kinds of companions appear to be distinguished. One way concerns the role of eroticism. Our assumption is that love includes it and friendship does not, but this is too crude a distinction to be useful in an area as complex and rich as relationship, there being more variations of passion and sexual behavior within each category than between the categories. The other way of distinguishing seems to assign demonstrating of relationship to love and maintaining of relationship to friendship. Three examples of this occur in our Western tradition. In love the other person tends to be seen as being the whole world, whereas in friendship the other person tends to be seen as the support for the whole world: love eclipses everything else; friendship offers a perspective on everything else. In love our style is that of a metaphor and poetry, whereas in friendship our style is that of honesty and essay. Love is extremist and even involves mutual lying; friendship is frankness and involves mutual exposure. Love is seen as loss of control with the threat of emotion disappearing; friendship, as responsibility with the threat of betrayal. In love we stress passion, whereas in friendship we stress loyalty. These typical conclusions can be explored as seeing love as the element of demonstrating relationship and seeing friendship as the element of maintaining it. But both elements belong in every companionship. If we make such distinctions at all between love and friendship, we should conclude that there is a time and place in a specific relationship for the attributes of love to prevail, another time and place for those of friendship to rule, and still another for a balance of them to occur. Our focus on the distinctions between lovers and friends has been overdone, but it can be useful as a reminder to love our friends and be friendly with our loved ones— to both demonstrate and maintain our companions.

To explore our love and friendship relations with regard to developing points us in another and more useful direction. When we accompany each other, development can be of three kinds: growth of mutuality, growth by spiraling through the three conditions, and growth into new relationships. Friends and lovers are valuable to us in their own right, but equally valuable as beginning a process of moving us beyond them. Ideally, when a companionship is fully established and mature, the partners move both separately and together into the world. This does not happen immediately. Our momentous discovery that another human being or a thing actually and truly exists, and that therefore, we also fully exist, is but a prelude to joining the human race. It is actually a movement from being an I-person to being an I-You-person. And pairs of lovers and groups of friends can remain that way. They can shut out the rest of the world and rely exclusively on themselves. Or they can lose themselves in society, trying to ignore difficulties in their relationships or to shore them up. The second movement involves becoming the full I-We-person. Our movement beyond love and friendship is a movement into plurality, from the one to the many. Love and friendship should be the two become one in order that the two and one may relate to the many.

There are two images that simply depict the two stages of our loves and friendships: the closed, round dance of the couple and the open, forward walk of the couple. In the beginning, the two persons face each other, holding hands and forming a tiny circle. In this composition, it is natural and easy to embrace and dance, but it is not natural and easy to walk long distances together, for the two look in opposite directions and one of them has to walk backward, guided totally by the other. In the second stage, the two persons are side by side, each holding only one hand of the other. They can see each other and move at will into an embrace, but they can both see where they are going and can move in that direction easily and naturally. Moreover, each has a free hand which can clasp the hand of someone else. This second image does not leave the first one behind, and so a complex pattern of movement emerges that graphically depicts fully developed relationship. At one moment the pair are walking together side by side, each holding hands with another as well. Then they drop each other's hands and walk with the other person, all still moving in roughly the same direction. Then the four rejoin hands, walking together again. Perhaps then the couple let go of those on the outside and join hands together for a little dance. The variety of possible

patterns is unlimited. They all stem from the two positions that are
equally useful and necessary—the closed, round dance of the couple
and the open, forward walk of the couple. When both images have
been combined into choreographed movement, the lovers or friends
have mutuality with each other and beyond.

These images say something about mature companionship, but do
not indicate anything about the other persons with whom we hold
hands or about how this hand-holding comes into being. We reach
for two kinds of new strangers—relatives and neighbors. We do the
reaching by means of two kinds of social projects—creating a family
and creating a community. One kind of movement has the social
project of reproduction—having and raising children and fostering
kinship. The pair is facing and moving toward society in doing this
project of continuing humanity. The movement involves an acceptance of the past and future generations. To care for a representative
of a new generation is to see and join the generations, and this is a
mutual confirmation of both the pair and the race as worthwhile.
Further, as parents, we discover our own parents and other kinfolk,
and also the relatives of our companions. What is involved is our care
for society by means of relatives and the generations. The other kind
of movement has the social project of production—having activities
in social groups and fostering community. Here we consider not just
those who live nearby and not even people who are physically present. Neighbors are all those we relate to other than kin—casual
acquaintances, associates, comrades, and good friends. These are psy-
chic neighbors. Each one of us is a participant in several networks of
them, because to be and have a companion is to experience the
networks of the companion. In attending fully to another human
being, we attend to his or her relationships and discover community
—the companions of companions. What is involved is our care for
society by means of friends of our friends and the various networks
involved.

The basic conclusion about companionship here is that full mutuality between two persons is exposure to and acceptance of the relationships of the other. These new strangers may be kinfolk or neighbors. Obviously we can and do face society in both ways, as creating
family and creating community; these are not in opposition and can
complement and support each other. In either case, we are moved
beyond the pair per se to welcome strangers. What is important about
our companionships is not the differences in how we face each other

as friends or lovers, but the differences in how we together face the rest of the world. The major issue is simply whether or not our companionships face only inward or also outward. As companions we must hold hands with each other, but also with relatives and neighbors, and also with their relatives and neighbors.

Now it is appropriate for us to look at our own close relationships and how they are oriented toward the rest of the world.

1. List the names of those who are close to you, those you love, and those who are your most intimate friends.
2. Write the name of one of the above persons to indicate a relationship that is too exclusive, too turned away from society. Indicate in what way.
3. Write the name of one of the above persons to indicate a relationship that is too merged, lost in the collectivity of a larger group. Indicate in what way.
4. In which way do you tend most to move with another toward society? Family and relatives. Neighbors and community. Both equally.
5. In what ways, if any, do you have problems in your relationships with any listed above regarding these two kinds of movement? List the names and briefly note the problems.

## Other Strangers

Welcoming strangers is hospitality. The early meanings of such terms as "hospital," "hospice," and "hospitable" combine in a suggestive way to provide a rich definition. Hospitality is a response to all strangers, travelers, and disadvantaged which involves receiving, entertaining, and caring for with generous kindness. The focus is on the alien—those human beings and things which do not fit into our lives as familiars. The challenge is to receive them, demonstrating our perception of them as companions; to entertain them, that is, attend to them, maintaining the relationship; and to care for them, seeing and responding to their plights, developing the relationship through response to their needs. This is welcoming strangers. Hospitality is not dusting off the living room furniture in order to please a guest for afternoon tea. It is more like inviting an enemy into one's tent and not killing the person on the premises, with the hope that you will not be killed either. Yet this courageous action is natural, the begin-

ning as well as the end of human behavior. Since we are all strange
to one another in a variety of ways, we are in existence only because
of the hospitality we have received. Our own first step into it occurs
with those we are the most intimate with—parents and siblings,
lovers and friends. Our second step into it happens with those next
familiar—relatives and neighbors. The third step can happen with all
that is quite unfamiliar to us—the complete strangers we meet. We
know only old strangers, new strangers, and complete strangers. In
each step, we encounter, tolerate, and enjoy the strange. We conclude
our discussion by exploring this hospitality as the demonstrating of
relationship by means of compassion, the maintaining of relationship
by means of employment, and the developing of relationship by
means of awe. The point made is that our companionship involves
ethical and social responsibilities, and that these, rather than being
onerous by nature and imposed upon us by exterior demands, are the
natural and pleasurable responsiveness proper to us.

The first of the three elements of hospitality is the most commonly
mentioned and the most impossible to accept—demonstrating relationship with strangers by means of compassion. Compassion is a
"crying out with those who suffer" that involves solidarity, consolation, and comfort.[62] Solidarity requires our breaking through the
differences between us, going beyond the alien, to define them and
ourselves by our similarities. Compassion means "to suffer with" and
occurs only when we give thanks that we are, in fact, like other
human beings. Consolation is the acceptance of suffering and a sharing of it. It is not a covering up of suffering, a false cheering of others,
or seeing our own pain in others, but being with the other where he
or she actually is. Such sharing can often even deepen awareness of
pain. And then comfort occurs which is "strength together." This
consequence of solidarity and consolation is a surprising strength
out of weakness. Mutual vulnerability does not eliminate suffering
and loneliness, but gives strength to confront it together. Solidarity,
consolation, and comfort are the ingredients of that compassion we
are to have for strangers who are in need.

Such compassion is possible because strangers can become companions; if this were not the case, we would have no companions.
However, not all strangers do become our companions and some even
become enemies. So our compassion tends to be reserved for our
closest intimates, for those who are seen as similar and familiar. Our
enjoyment of the similar is a natural and beneficial tendency which

makes our relationships possible and preserves them. For like to seek like is invaluable and enjoyable. But for like to seek only like, and worse, to attempt to fashion unlike into like, is destructive. This is so because it is also natural and beneficial for us to seek the unlike, to open ourselves up to the unfamiliar and the surprising. It is only the rule of like seeking like that is destructive. Further, we know that this reign destroys relationships with our intimates as well. So compassion for strangers is necessary and possible. Only a false piety sees it as a disregard of self. It is a capacity necessary for survival granted by evolution and sustained by culture. But what is necessary and possible is not necessarily sufficient. Demonstrating our relationship may let us rest too much in ease in affection with a stranger. Compassion does become romantic foolishness when we rely upon it exclusively.

With strangers as well as with friends, maintaining relationship occurs by means of mutual employment—using and being used. It is valuable because it can occur either before or after compassion. Strangers and even enemies frequently experience no compassion but do enter into involvements as their country's ambassadors, business associates, and community acquaintances. It is an alternative to competition and warfare. Strange bedfellows are of value. Mutual employment prevents us from focusing on the moments of empathy idealistically and, ultimately, despairingly. Yet it is even more valuable in its own right. Employment is a variety of gift exchange.[63] It involves the obligations of giving, receiving, and repaying. Those of us who spend much time with strangers are constantly involved with giving and receiving innumerable small favors—drinks, meals, tickets. We do the same in relationships with the formerly strange. Gifts are not outgrown, because compassion is not constant and not sufficient anyway. The gifts bind us. We may tend to see a debt as a burden to be eliminated, but this is impossible unless we choose to exist either in isolation or in competition. Relationships cannot exist without capacity and willingness to give and receive gifts. To be out of debt is to be dead. Debt is a burden only when the process is stopped and exchange cannot continue. This is the unbearable problem that causes withdrawal or warfare. Further, it happens most often when we see ourselves as having nothing to give. We do not mind receiving if we can be confident of returning. Can you remember occasions in which you received and could not return and the relationship was damaged? Most of us can recall when we could not repay. We are not likely to be so alert to the occasions in which others cannot repay. How are we to welcome strangers, both those familiar and those unfamiliar to us? We welcome them by facilitating their participation in the gift exchange with us. At every level of our community and in society as a whole, we need both to foster understanding of what acceptable gifts are and to promote opportunity for everyone to have such gifts to give. Hospitality is not just giving and not just graciously receiving as well, but also acting to help the stranger possess a gift to give. We are referring to ways of using and being used. We survive by means of freely given compassion, but also by interchange of usage which binds us together regardless of empathy.

Hospitality toward strangers includes developing relationship and occurs by means of awe. I have already said that religious revelation is revelation of a relationship which proclaims that relationship is. But revelation is also revelation of the strange, a meeting with the uncommon, uncanny, and unexpected. These two conclusions together make a third: relationship is with the strange. Hospitality— the welcoming of strangers—is not the exception but the norm. A full relationship is with the strange and surprising. To meet anyone or anything is dumbfounding. Our response to true meeting is awe. Another way to express this is to observe the obvious fact that we cannot have a relationship with ourselves but only with someone or something else. What is strange is simply whatever or whoever is quite other than us. Strangeness is omnipresent, but we may not see it because we are doing our best to see only ourselves and, therefore, everyone and everything else as extensions of ourselves, and that which can be perfectly ordered and understood by ourselves. But careful and caring attention to what is common, domestic, and familiar for us will allow a breakthrough in which the alien reappears. Most of us will flee most of the time. Fortunately the occasions for recognition of the strange are nearly always, and our chances to welcome strangers abound. When we take a chance, true meeting occurs, and our response is awe.

This awe is the response that keeps us open to the strange. We should recognize and cherish it. Maintaining our awe is a keeping of the faith. Awe supported in this way becomes respect. The term "respect" is derived from the Latin verb meaning "to look back." To respect something or someone is to fully perceive it. Respect is sustained acknowledgment of the strange. Not just passive, it is a commitment to the world experienced as strange. Finally, when respect is not only sustained but also actively directed, it becomes vision. Vision is extraordinary sight, the capacity not just to see the strange when relationship occurs, but to move toward what will be experienced as strange. Vision seeks out the strange. So we have a possible pattern of response that can assist our relationships. Awe is the first stage, being our response to the experience of the strange. The second stage is the sustaining of this awe which can engender respect. The third stage is the sustaining of respect which can engender vision. Awe is the passive response to the strange, respect is the active commitment to the strange, and vision is the creative search for the strange. So our hospitality is developed in a relationship by the nurturing of our awe into respect and vision.

Discussions of relationship tend to dwell on the exceptional moments that occur. Much of our lives in relationships are unexceptional. Moreover, they are often routinely disappointing, and sometimes just wearing or worn out. Even so, there are occasions when we are surprised by relationships with total strangers or by the intimate strangers we live with. Although we should not let these experiences represent all that is involved, it is crucial to note them and be reminded of their influence over us.

1. Recall an experience of compassion with a total, or nearly total, stranger.
2. Recall an experience of compassion with a familiar stranger (lover, friend, relative, neighbor, etc.).
3. Recall an experience of mutual employment with a total, or nearly total, stranger.
4. Recall an experience of mutual employment with a familiar stranger.
5. Recall an experience of awe with a total, or nearly total, stranger.
6. Recall an experience of awe with a familiar stranger.
7. What do you enjoy most in your experiences of welcoming strangers?
8. What do you enjoy least in your experiences of welcoming strangers?
9. What problems do you have in your welcoming of strangers?
10. Note one or more possibilities for welcoming a stranger that you might act upon.

When our compassion and mutual employment are accompanied by the developing of awe, respect, and vision, our pride of seeing others as only like ourselves is replaced by our humility of realizing that others see us as strange. And to know we are seen by others as strange and yet welcomed by them elicits our awe and contributes to it. Welcoming strangers involves entering into the conditions of loneliness, solitude, and companionship, never resting long in one of them but living on the move. Welcoming strangers involves increasing forays into the realms of relationships, encountering new individuals, new groups of people, new representatives of the generations, new objects, and new experiences of the world as a whole. It is the occurrence of the strange in these conditions and realms which keeps us moving. This movement is life. The infant who sees his mother is the father of the adult visionary. The mother is strange as well as familiar. Still, a smile is in order. The infant has to smile at the stranger in order to survive humanly, as a member of the world of relationship. Looking at each other, and at all others both amazed and amused, we give and receive life.

# NOTES

1. Harry Stack Sullivan, *The Interpersonal Theory of Psychiatry*, ed. by Helen S. Perry and Mary L. Gawel (W. W. Norton & Co., 1953), p. 260.

2. Ibid.

3. Robert S. Weiss, ed., *Loneliness: The Experience of Emotional and Social Isolation* (M.I.T. Press, 1974), p. 11.

4. These statements are from students at Union Theological Seminary.

5. These words and statements are from students at Union Theological Seminary and from participants in church study groups.

6. Robert Frost, "An Old Man's Winter Night," *Robert Frost's Poems*, ed. by Louis Untermeyer (Washington Square Press, 1946), p. 118.

7. Theodore Roethke, *Straw for the Fire: From the Notebooks of Theodore Roethke*, ed. by David Wagoner (Doubleday & Co., 1972), p. 32.

8. Eithne Tabor, *The Cliff's Edge: Songs of a Psychotic* (Sheed & Ward, 1950), p. 36.

9. Elizabeth Jennings, "Absence," *A Sense of the World* (Holt, Rinehart & Winston, 1959), p. 35.

10. Jaber F. Gubrium, *The Myth of the Golden Years* (Charles C Thomas, Publisher, 1973), pp. 116ff.

11. Carson McCullers, *The Member of the Wedding* (New Directions, 1963), pp. 51–52.

12. Sullivan, *The Interpersonal Theory of Psychiatry*, p. 290.

13. Richard H. Williams and Claudine G. Wirth, *Lives Through the Years: Styles of Life and Successful Aging* (Atherton Press, 1965).

14. Willard Gaylin, ed., *The Meaning of Despair* (Science House, 1968).

15. Peter Marris, *Loss and Change* (Doubleday & Co., Anchor Books, 1975).

16. Clark E. Moustakas, *Loneliness* (Prentice-Hall, 1961).

17. Some of these examples have been taken from a discussion by Jane

Pearce and Saul Newton, *The Conditions of Human Growth* (Citadel Press, 1969), pp. 170ff.

18. Moustakas, *Loneliness,* p. 101.

19. Weiss, *Loneliness,* pp. 17–22.

20. Avery D. Weissman and Thomas P. Hackett, "Predilection to Death," in *Death and Identity,* rev. ed. by Robert Fulton (Charles Press Publishers, 1976), p. 301.

21. G. K. Chesterton, *Orthodoxy* (London: Bodley Head, 1949), p. 4.

22. Theodore Isaac Rubin, *Cat* (Ballantine Books, 1966).

23. May Sarton, *Journal of a Solitude* (W. W. Norton & Co., 1977).

24. Ibid., p. 81.

25. William Wordsworth, "The Daffodils," in *Concise Treasury of Great Poems,* ed. by Louis Untermeyer (Pocket Books, 1973), p. 210.

26. May Sarton, "The Rewards of Living a Solitary Life," *The New York Times* (April 8, 1974), contained in *To Be Alone: The Sweet and the Bittersweet,* compiled by Joan Berg (Crown Publishers, 1974), p. 32.

27. Sarton, *Journal of a Solitude,* p. 11.

28. Weiss, *Loneliness,* p. 14.

29. Jonathan Swift, quoted by Herbert Prochnow, *The Public Speaker's Treasure Chest* (Harper & Brothers, 1942), p. 368. No source given.

30. George Bernard Shaw, *The Doctor's Dilemma* (Penguin Books, 1965), p. 177.

31. Henry David Thoreau, *Walden* (Thomas Y. Crowell Co., 1966), p. 170.

32. Ibid., p. 365.

33. Alfred North Whitehead, *Religion in the Making* (Macmillan Co., 1926), pp. 16–17, 60.

34. Thomas Merton, *Thoughts in Solitude* (Farrar, Straus & Giroux, 1976), p. 101.

35. Ibid., p. 85.

36. Ibid., p. 113.

37. Florida Scott-Maxwell, *The Measure of My Days* (Alfred A. Knopf, 1973), pp. 80–81.

38. Thoreau, *Walden,* p. 176.

39. Richard E. Byrd, *Alone* (G. P. Putnam's Sons, 1938).

40. Ibid., pp. 154–155.

41. Ibid., p. 85.

42. Peter Handke, *The Left-Handed Woman,* in *Two Novels by Peter Handke,* tr. by Ralph Mannheim (Avon Books, 1979).

43. Thomas Wolfe, "God's Lonely Man," in *The Hills Beyond* (New American Library, Signet Classics, 1968), p. 148.

44. Sarton, *Journal of a Solitude,* pp. 31–32.

45. Scott-Maxwell, *The Measure of My Days.*

46. Ibid., p. 15.

47. Ibid.

48. Sarton, *Journal of a Solitude,* pp. 44–45.

49. Ibid., p. 44.

50. Wolfe, *The Hills Beyond,* p. 154.

51. Bernice L. Neugarten, "The Awareness of Middle Age," in *Middle Age and Aging,* ed. by Neugarten (University of Chicago Press, 1972), p. 98.

52. Doris Lessing, *The Summer Before the Dark* (Alfred A. Knopf, 1974).

53. Sullivan, *The Interpersonal Theory of Psychiatry,* pp. 245–256.

54. Pearce and Newton, *The Conditions of Human Growth,* pp. 105–106.

55. Ibid., p. 106.

56. Ibid., pp. 217–218.

57. Jean-Paul Sartre, "Drôle d'Amitié," *Les Temps Moderns,* Vol. 5, Part 1, Nos. 49 and 50 (Nov. and Dec. 1949), pp. 769–806, 1009–1039. Tr. by Maurice Friedman, summarized and quoted by him in his *To Deny Our Nothingness* (University of Chicago Press, 1978), pp. 375–376.

58. Marjorie Fiske Lowenthal, Majda Thurnher, David Chiriboga, *Four Stages of Life* (Jossey-Bass, 1975), Ch. 3.

59. Pearce and Newton, *The Conditions of Human Growth,* p. 222.

60. Ibid., p. 223.

61. Ibid., pp. 217–227.

62. Henri Nouwen, "Compassion: Solidarity, Consolation and Comfort," *America,* Mar. 13, 1976, pp. 195–196.

63. Marcel Mauss, *The Gift: Forms and Functions of Exchange in Archaic Societies,* tr. by Ian Cunnison (W. W. Norton & Co., 1967).